Everyday Happy

A journal for happiness

Emma O'Connor

Dedication

This book was written for my sons,
Daniel and Rory

And for

YOU!

"Everything that is or was began with a dream."

Lavagirl, *The Adventures of Sharkboy and Lavagirl*

Acknowledgements

Thank you to my children for inspiring this book, and to my husband for supporting me.

Thank you to the other children and families for sharing their stories with me, and reminding me to keep writing.

Thank you to the researchers, scientists, psychologists and happiness experts for sharing their knowledge and giving me the tools to help my son.

Disclaimer

Please remember that while this book is designed to provide a helping hand as you walk yourself back to happiness, it does not claim to be a replacement for qualified psychological or medical treatment.

Table of Contents

Introduction

When I was 10 years old, I forgot how to 'be happy'. I spent the next few years feeling worried or anxious about... EVERYTHING. I worried about all the normal stuff like homework and having friends, but I also worried a lot about what people thought of me, and felt embarrassed, ashamed and frightened most of the time. Of course, people weren't thinking about me nearly as much as I thought, but because I was so overwhelmed with negative emotions I didn't realise. I also didn't realise that it didn't matter what other people thought anyway, what mattered was how I felt about myself.
I needed to realise that happiness was available to me.
I needed to learn how to do happy, and that my happiness was up to me!
Now I am a mum, and I have a son who has been worried. I decided I didn't want him to spend all those years feeling bad like I did, so I wrote this book to help him, and I hope it can help you too.

Who is this for?

"Clap along if you feel like happiness is for you."

Pharrell Williams, *Happy*

If you are feeling sad, anxious, depressed, or worried and can't seem to walk your way back to happiness, this journal can help you do it. Or if you just like the idea of being happier and making the most of every day, this journal is also for you.

Life is supposed to be fun! When we're very young happiness is something we seem to know how to do. When something goes wrong we get upset, but then we have a cuddle, play with our toys, or go outside. We do something to feel better.
But somehow, at some stage in our lives, many of us forget how to be happy! How to DO happy!
In this book we are going to focus completely on happiness, so rather than looking at 'the problems' or 'where things went wrong' (there are plenty of books about that), our focus is going to be on what is going RIGHT, what we can DO to make things better, and how we CAN be happy.

What is happiness?

Happiness is tricky to define because it is very different for everyone. It's made out to be something we should feel, but can't until we accomplish success, fame, friendships, lots of money, or own the next piece of tech. By the way, there is nothing wrong with any of these things, they just won't necessarily 'make' you happy. The state of being happy is described in terms of joy, contentment, pleasure, and satisfaction, but how do we achieve it? And what about the idea that we should just BE HAPPY, NOW, with what we 'have'?
Well here's the thing: nothing outside of you will give you lasting happiness...

The Happiness needs to come from you.

Why be happy?

Well, there's a good question! It is becoming accepted that the happier you are, the better your life will be (sounds obvious I know...). Dr Christine Carter, the author of *Raising Happiness* (2011), says that happy people are 'more successful' and also 'tend to be healthier and live longer'. It turns out that you can be more creative, intelligent, energetic, resilient, and have better friendships, just from being happy! You'll probably also end up better able to cope with stress, challenges and negative emotions when they show up (more on that later). All of this added together can lead to better career and financial prospects!

In fact, learning how to be happy will empower you, and give you the confidence to follow your heart and become the person you really want to be!

How do I do it then?

Here's the secret... You don't get to be happy by coincidence, or through success, or because someone or something 'made' you happy. Happiness, true happiness, is a bunch of small decisions; the combination of your habits and your beliefs; the stuff you DO, THINK and SAY (to other people and yourself) EVERY DAY!
In other words happiness is a choice, your choice.

Here's How…

Positive psychologists say that there are certain habits, or specific things you can do every day (or as often as possible) that will increase your level of happiness. Some important ones are:
1. Being Grateful. Writing down things that you're thankful for, every day.
2. Remembering the good stuff. Write in your journal about the good that has happened that day.
3. Meditating. Sitting quietly and relaxing.
4. Being kind. Giving your time or energy to help others.
5. Getting some exercise. Choosing fun ways to get active.
6. Nurturing strong and happy relationships.
7. Doing things you love.
8. Learning new things.

Hint
Doing just one of these every day will help you.

Shawn Achor (2011), *The Happy Secret to Better Work.* TED.com
Positive Psychology and the Science of Happiness (ND), www.pursuit-of-happiness.org

---

How to use this book

This journal will help you create your own habits for happiness. There are plenty of ideas for you to use every day to help make yourself happier.

Remember, this is not rocket science (although if you like rocket science definitely do some!). The activities in here are easy, but to benefit from them you have to DO them! And do as many as you can as often as you can. (Don't worry though, it's supposed to be fun.)

You will find loads of information throughout this book on all kinds of topics related to happiness. You don't have to read it all (although you can); you can just read the bits that suit you!
There are 365 happy days in here, enough for a whole year.
But you don't have to take a year, you can take as long as you like. That's why there are no dates. Start when you like, and fill your days with happy habits as often as you like.

Hint
This book is for you and about you! Fill it up with your stuff, thoughts, feelings, drawings and photos. Anything that brings you happiness!

Let's get started

Firstly: Set your happiness goal: define your version of happiness. Use a pencil as it may change over time!

Then, every day (or as often as you can):

In the morning...

1. Look at your journal and fill in the 'I am grateful for...' section. This will help you start your day seeing positives. Try and write three new things every day.

2. Make a plan (with your family) to tick as many boxes in the 'tick box' section as you can that day. (Aim for at least the first three.)

3. Go and have a great day!

In the evening...

4. Tick your boxes.

5. Write about a part of your day that you really enjoyed.

6. Rate your happiness.

GO FOR IT!

My happiness goal is...

Hint
Set a positive goal!

Setting (and reaching) goals for happiness

If setting (and reaching) your happiness goal seems tricky, here are a few tips to help you.

1. Set a goal that is important to you. Ask yourself questions like:
'Why do I want to be happier?'
'What situations do I want to be happier in?'
'Who do I want a happier friendship/relationship with?'(Friends, parents, yourself.)

2. Enjoy the ride.
This journal will take you on a journey towards your happiness. While it's important to keep the end goal in sight, it's also a great idea to enjoy the small steps that will take you there.

3. Be positive.
Write your goal down in a positive way. Stating what you want (rather than what you don't) will give you the motivation to keep going.

4. Ride the wave.
Everyone has ups and downs, so don't freak out if you feel yourself drop. Just keep going. Your path to happiness is a bit like climbing a mountain: the skills and habits you learn will become your anchor points to stop you falling too far down. Just keep going. If the path looks too difficult, find a different way around. Just keep going!

Nadia Goodman (2014), *The Science of Setting Goals.*
Ideas.ted.com

—

Day 1

I am grateful for:

1...

....

2...

....

3...

....

Today I:

[] Did 15 minutes of exercise
[] Sat quietly and relaxed (meditation)
[] Was kind to someone.
How?...
[] Spent time in nature
[] Listened to my favourite song
[] Ate something healthy
[] Called a friend
[] Hugged someone
[] Completed an unfinished task. What was
   it?.......................................
[] Started/worked on a hobby
[] Read a few pages of a great book
[] Took photos of something beautiful
[] Started to learn a new skill
[] Laughed at something really funny

Today was fun
because.......................................
....
....

Happiness rating:

        1 2 3 4 5 6 7 8 9 10

Day 2

I am grateful for:
1...
....
2...
....
3...
....

Today I:

[] Did 15 minutes of exercise
[] Sat quietly and relaxed (meditation)
[] Was kind to someone.
How?...
[] Spent time in nature
[] Listened to my favourite song
[] Ate something healthy
[] Called a friend
[] Hugged someone
[] Completed an unfinished task. What was
    it?..
[] Started/worked on a hobby
[] Read a few pages of a great book
[] Took photos of something beautiful
[] Started to learn a new skill
[] Laughed at something really funny

Today was fun
because..
....
....

Happiness rating:

        1 2 3 4 5 6 7 8 9 10

11

Day 3

I am grateful for:
1..
....
2..
....
3..
....

Today I:

[] Did 15 minutes of exercise
[] Sat quietly and relaxed (meditation)
[] Was kind to someone.
How?...
[] Spent time in nature
[] Listened to my favourite song
[] Ate something healthy
[] Called a friend
[] Hugged someone
[] Completed an unfinished task. What was
   it?..
[] Started/worked on a hobby
[] Read a few pages of a great book
[] Took photos of something beautiful
[] Started to learn a new skill
[] Laughed at something really funny

Today was fun
because..
....
....

Happiness rating:

    1 2 3 4 5 6 7 8 9 10

Day 4

I am grateful for:

1...
....

2...
....

3...
....

Today I:

[] Did 15 minutes of exercise
[] Sat quietly and relaxed (meditation)
[] Was kind to someone.
How?.......................................
[] Spent time in nature
[] Listened to my favourite song
[] Ate something healthy
[] Called a friend
[] Hugged someone
[] Completed an unfinished task. What was
   it?.....................................
[] Started/worked on a hobby
[] Read a few pages of a great book
[] Took photos of something beautiful
[] Started to learn a new skill
[] Laughed at something really funny

Today was fun
because....................................
....
....

Happiness rating:

   1 2 3 4 5 6 7 8 9 10

Day 5

I am grateful for:

1..
....
2..
....
3..
....

Today I:

[] Did 15 minutes of exercise
[] Sat quietly and relaxed (meditation)
[] Was kind to someone.
How?......................................
[] Spent time in nature
[] Listened to my favourite song
[] Ate something healthy
[] Called a friend
[] Hugged someone
[] Completed an unfinished task. What was
    it?....................................
[] Started/worked on a hobby
[] Read a few pages of a great book
[] Took photos of something beautiful
[] Started to learn a new skill
[] Laughed at something really funny

Today was fun
because...................................
....
....

Happiness rating:

    1 2 3 4 5 6 7 8 9 10

Day 6

I am grateful for:

1...
....

2...
....

3...
....

Today I:

[] Did 15 minutes of exercise
[] Sat quietly and relaxed (meditation)
[] Was kind to someone.
How?...
[] Spent time in nature
[] Listened to my favourite song
[] Ate something healthy
[] Called a friend
[] Hugged someone
[] Completed an unfinished task. What was
    it?...
[] Started/worked on a hobby
[] Read a few pages of a great book
[] Took photos of something beautiful
[] Started to learn a new skill
[] Laughed at something really funny

Today was fun
because...
....
....

Happiness rating:

        1 2 3 4 5 6 7 8 9 10

Day 7

I am grateful for:

1..

....

2..

....

3..

....

Today I:

[] Did 15 minutes of exercise
[] Sat quietly and relaxed (meditation)
[] Was kind to someone.
How?..
[] Spent time in nature
[] Listened to my favourite song
[] Ate something healthy
[] Called a friend
[] Hugged someone
[] Completed an unfinished task. What was
   it?..
[] Started/worked on a hobby
[] Read a few pages of a great book
[] Took photos of something beautiful
[] Started to learn a new skill
[] Laughed at something really funny

Today was fun
because..

....

....

Happiness rating:

1 2 3 4 5 6 7 8 9 10

"You are the most talented, most interesting, most extraordinary person in the universe. You are capable of amazing things."

The Lego Movie

Day 8

I am grateful for:
1..
....
2..
....
3..
....

Today I:

[] Did 15 minutes of exercise
[] Sat quietly and relaxed (meditation)
[] Was kind to someone.
How?...
[] Spent time in nature
[] Listened to my favourite song
[] Ate something healthy
[] Called a friend
[] Hugged someone
[] Completed an unfinished task. What was
   it?...
[] Started/worked on a hobby
[] Read a few pages of a great book
[] Took photos of something beautiful
[] Started to learn a new skill
[] Laughed at something really funny

Today was fun
because..
....
....

Happiness rating:

        1 2 3 4 5 6 7 8 9 10

Day 9

I am grateful for:

1...
....

2...
....

3...
....

Today I:

[] Did 15 minutes of exercise
[] Sat quietly and relaxed (meditation)
[] Was kind to someone.
How?..
[] Spent time in nature
[] Listened to my favourite song
[] Ate something healthy
[] Called a friend
[] Hugged someone .
[] Completed an unfinished task. What was
   it?......................................
[] Started/worked on a hobby
[] Read a few pages of a great book
[] Took photos of something beautiful
[] Started to learn a new skill
[] Laughed at something really funny

Today was fun
because.....................................
....
....

Happiness rating:

    1 2 3 4 5 6 7 8 9 10

Day 10

I am grateful for:

1..
....

2..
....

3..
....

Today I:

[] Did 15 minutes of exercise
[] Sat quietly and relaxed (meditation)
[] Was kind to someone.
How?...
[] Spent time in nature
[] Listened to my favourite song
[] Ate something healthy
[] Called a friend
[] Hugged someone
[] Completed an unfinished task. What was
    it?..
[] Started/worked on a hobby
[] Read a few pages of a great book
[] Took photos of something beautiful
[] Started to learn a new skill
[] Laughed at something really funny

Today was fun
because.......................................
....
....

Happiness rating:

      1 2 3 4 5 6 7 8 9 10

Day 11

I am grateful for:

1...
....

2...
....

3...
....

Today I:

[] Did 15 minutes of exercise
[] Sat quietly and relaxed (meditation)
[] Was kind to someone.
How?...
[] Spent time in nature
[] Listened to my favourite song
[] Ate something healthy
[] Called a friend
[] Hugged someone
[] Completed an unfinished task. What was
   it?..
[] Started/worked on a hobby
[] Read a few pages of a great book
[] Took photos of something beautiful
[] Started to learn a new skill
[] Laughed at something really funny

Today was fun
because..
....
....

Happiness rating:

     1 2 3 4 5 6 7 8 9 10

Day 12

I am grateful for:
1..
....
2..
....
3..
....

Today I:

[] Did 15 minutes of exercise
[] Sat quietly and relaxed (meditation)
[] Was kind to someone.
How?..
[] Spent time in nature
[] Listened to my favourite song
[] Ate something healthy
[] Called a friend
[] Hugged someone
[] Completed an unfinished task. What was
   it?.....................................
[] Started/worked on a hobby
[] Read a few pages of a great book
[] Took photos of something beautiful
[] Started to learn a new skill
[] Laughed at something really funny

Today was fun
because......................................
....
....

Happiness rating:

1 2 3 4 5 6 7 8 9 10

Day 13

I am grateful for:

1...
....

2...
....

3...
....

Today I:

[] Did 15 minutes of exercise
[] Sat quietly and relaxed (meditation)
[] Was kind to someone.
How?.......................................
[] Spent time in nature
[] Listened to my favourite song
[] Ate something healthy
[] Called a friend
[] Hugged someone
[] Completed an unfinished task. What was
    it?.....................................
[] Started/worked on a hobby
[] Read a few pages of a great book
[] Took photos of something beautiful
[] Started to learn a new skill
[] Laughed at something really funny

Today was fun
because....................................
....
....

Happiness rating:

    1 2 3 4 5 6 7 8 9 10

Day 14

I am grateful for:

1...
....

2...
....

3...
....

Today I:

[] Did 15 minutes of exercise
[] Sat quietly and relaxed (meditation)
[] Was kind to someone.
How?.......................................
[] Spent time in nature
[] Listened to my favourite song
[] Ate something healthy
[] Called a friend
[] Hugged someone
[] Completed an unfinished task. What was
   it?......................................
[] Started/worked on a hobby
[] Read a few pages of a great book
[] Took photos of something beautiful
[] Started to learn a new skill
[] Laughed at something really funny

Today was fun
because.....................................
....
....

Happiness rating:

     1 2 3 4 5 6 7 8 9 10

Gratitude Rocks...

Practising gratitude is one of the most powerful steps towards happiness. It is the conscious recognition of the good you receive in your life, and can help you appreciate and notice what you have, instead of what you don't.

This act of 'appreciating' can actually start to train your brain to automatically look for positives.
Shawn Achor (2011), *The Happy Secret to Better work.* TED.com

You may even notice that feeling grateful actively brings more positives into your life.

Appreciating the things people have done for you can lead to stronger friendships and make you feel more connected to others. Feeling grateful can also help you deal with stress and negative emotions.

Gratitude is more than just being thankful when things have gone right (that's just too easy!). The gratitude that will bring you lasting happiness is the everyday type. It is noticing and being thankful for the little (or big) blessings every single day; things that are easy to take for granted, like having a healthy body, warm house and yummy food, your family, friends, and even your stuff! It is also (hard as it is) searching for the good in difficult or challenging situations. How did it make you better or stronger? And what did you learn?

According to Dr Emmons, author of *Thanks! How The New Science of Gratitude Can Make You Happier*, deciding to be grateful every day can significantly increase your happiness, as well as improve your creativity, resilience, relationships AND give your immune system a boost.
In short an attitude of gratitude can bring success and happiness to many areas of your life!

HINT
Personally thanking someone for something they have done for you... Sending your teacher, friend, parent or relative a personal thank you note or email, or thanking them in person can make you, and them, happier!

"It is not happy people who are thankful. It is thankful people who are happy."

Unknown

Day 15

I am grateful for:

1..
....

2..
....

3..
....

Today I:

[] Did 15 minutes of exercise
[] Sat quietly and relaxed (meditation)
[] Was kind to someone.
How?..
[] Spent time in nature
[] Listened to my favourite song
[] Ate something healthy
[] Called a friend
[] Hugged someone
[] Completed an unfinished task. What was
   it?......................................
[] Started/worked on a hobby
[] Read a few pages of a great book
[] Took photos of something beautiful
[] Started to learn a new skill
[] Laughed at something really funny

Today was fun
because.....................................
....
....

Happiness rating:

        1 2 3 4 5 6 7 8 9 10

Day 16

I am grateful for:
1...
....
2...
....
3...
....

Today I:

[] Did 15 minutes of exercise
[] Sat quietly and relaxed (meditation)
[] Was kind to someone.
How?..
[] Spent time in nature
[] Listened to my favourite song
[] Ate something healthy
[] Called a friend
[] Hugged someone
[] Completed an unfinished task. What was
   it?..
[] Started/worked on a hobby
[] Read a few pages of a great book
[] Took photos of something beautiful
[] Started to learn a new skill
[] Laughed at something really funny

Today was fun
because.......................................
....
....

Happiness rating:

        1 2 3 4 5 6 7 8 9 10

Day 17

I am grateful for:
1..
....
2..
....
3..
....

Today I:

[] Did 15 minutes of exercise
[] Sat quietly and relaxed (meditation)
[] Was kind to someone.
How?...
[] Spent time in nature
[] Listened to my favourite song
[] Ate something healthy
[] Called a friend
[] Hugged someone
[] Completed an unfinished task. What was
    it?.......................................
[] Started/worked on a hobby
[] Read a few pages of a great book
[] Took photos of something beautiful
[] Started to learn a new skill
[] Laughed at something really funny

Today was fun
because......................................
....
....

Happiness rating:

        1   2   3   4   5   6   7   8   9   10

Day 18

I am grateful for:

1...
....

2...
....

3...
....

Today I:

[] Did 15 minutes of exercise
[] Sat quietly and relaxed (meditation)
[] Was kind to someone.
How?..
[] Spent time in nature
[] Listened to my favourite song
[] Ate something healthy
[] Called a friend
[] Hugged someone
[] Completed an unfinished task. What was
   it?..
[] Started/worked on a hobby
[] Read a few pages of a great book
[] Took photos of something beautiful
[] Started to learn a new skill
[] Laughed at something really funny

Today was fun
because...
....
....

Happiness rating:

     1 2 3 4 5 6 7 8 9 10

Day 19

I am grateful for:

1..
....

2..
....

3..
....

Today I:

[] Did 15 minutes of exercise
[] Sat quietly and relaxed (meditation)
[] Was kind to someone.
How?.....................................
[] Spent time in nature
[] Listened to my favourite song
[] Ate something healthy
[] Called a friend
[] Hugged someone
[] Completed an unfinished task. What was
   it?...................................
[] Started/worked on a hobby
[] Read a few pages of a great book
[] Took photos of something beautiful
[] Started to learn a new skill
[] Laughed at something really funny

Today was fun
because..................................
....
....

Happiness rating:

    1 2 3 4 5 6 7 8 9 10

Day 20

I am grateful for:

1..
....

2..
....

3..
....

Today I:

[] Did 15 minutes of exercise
[] Sat quietly and relaxed (meditation)
[] Was kind to someone.
How?...
[] Spent time in nature
[] Listened to my favourite song
[] Ate something healthy
[] Called a friend
[] Hugged someone
[] Completed an unfinished task. What was
   it?..
[] Started/worked on a hobby
[] Read a few pages of a great book
[] Took photos of something beautiful
[] Started to learn a new skill
[] Laughed at something really funny

Today was fun
because......................................
....
....

Happiness rating:

1 2 3 4 5 6 7 8 9 10

Day 21

I am grateful for:

1...
....

2...
....

3...
....

Today I:

[] Did 15 minutes of exercise
[] Sat quietly and relaxed (meditation)
[] Was kind to someone.
How?..
[] Spent time in nature
[] Listened to my favourite song
[] Ate something healthy
[] Called a friend
[] Hugged someone
[] Completed an unfinished task. What was
   it?......................................
[] Started/worked on a hobby
[] Read a few pages of a great book
[] Took photos of something beautiful
[] Started to learn a new skill
[] Laughed at something really funny

Today was fun
because......................................
....
....

Happiness rating:

          1 2 3 4 5 6 7 8 9 10

"You have brains in your head. You have feet in your shoes. You can steer yourself in any direction you choose."

Dr Seuss, *Oh, the Places You'll Go!*

Day 22

I am grateful for:
1..
....
2..
....
3..
....

Today I:

[] Did 15 minutes of exercise
[] Sat quietly and relaxed (meditation)
[] Was kind to someone.
How?..
[] Spent time in nature
[] Listened to my favourite song
[] Ate something healthy
[] Called a friend
[] Hugged someone
[] Completed an unfinished task. What was
    it?.......................................
[] Started/worked on a hobby
[] Read a few pages of a great book
[] Took photos of something beautiful
[] Started to learn a new skill
[] Laughed at something really funny

Today was fun
because.......................................
....
....

Happiness rating:

        1 2 3 4 5 6 7 8 9 10

Day 23

I am grateful for:

1..
....

2..
....

3..
....

Today I:

[] Did 15 minutes of exercise
[] Sat quietly and relaxed (meditation)
[] Was kind to someone.
How?.......................................
[] Spent time in nature
[] Listened to my favourite song
[] Ate something healthy
[] Called a friend
[] Hugged someone
[] Completed an unfinished task. What was
   it?......................................
[] Started/worked on a hobby
[] Read a few pages of a great book
[] Took photos of something beautiful
[] Started to learn a new skill
[] Laughed at something really funny

Today was fun
because...................................
....
....

Happiness rating:

        1 2 3 4 5 6 7 8 9 10

Day 24

I am grateful for:

1..
....

2..
....

3..
....

Today I:

[] Did 15 minutes of exercise
[] Sat quietly and relaxed (meditation)
[] Was kind to someone.
How?.......................................
[] Spent time in nature
[] Listened to my favourite song
[] Ate something healthy
[] Called a friend
[] Hugged someone
[] Completed an unfinished task. What was
    it?....................................
[] Started/worked on a hobby
[] Read a few pages of a great book
[] Took photos of something beautiful
[] Started to learn a new skill
[] Laughed at something really funny

Today was fun
because....................................
....
....

Happiness rating:

    1 2 3 4 5 6 7 8 9 10

Day 25

I am grateful for:
1..
....
2..
....
3..
....

Today I:

[] Did 15 minutes of exercise
[] Sat quietly and relaxed (meditation)
[] Was kind to someone.
How?..
[] Spent time in nature
[] Listened to my favourite song
[] Ate something healthy
[] Called a friend
[] Hugged someone
[] Completed an unfinished task. What was
   it?..
[] Started/worked on a hobby
[] Read a few pages of a great book
[] Took photos of something beautiful
[] Started to learn a new skill
[] Laughed at something really funny

Today was fun
because...
....
....

Happiness rating:

     1 2 3 4 5 6 7 8 9 10

Day 26

I am grateful for:

1...
....

2...
....

3...
....

Today I:

[] Did 15 minutes of exercise
[] Sat quietly and relaxed (meditation)
[] Was kind to someone.
How?...
[] Spent time in nature
[] Listened to my favourite song
[] Ate something healthy
[] Called a friend
[] Hugged someone
[] Completed an unfinished task. What was
    it?...
[] Started/worked on a hobby
[] Read a few pages of a great book
[] Took photos of something beautiful
[] Started to learn a new skill
[] Laughed at something really funny

Today was fun
because..
....
....

Happiness rating:

         1 2 3 4 5 6 7 8 9 10

Day 27

I am grateful for:

1...
....

2...
....

3...
....

Today I:

[] Did 15 minutes of exercise
[] Sat quietly and relaxed (meditation)
[] Was kind to someone.
How?...
[] Spent time in nature
[] Listened to my favourite song
[] Ate something healthy
[] Called a friend
[] Hugged someone
[] Completed an unfinished task. What was
   it?.......................................
[] Started/worked on a hobby
[] Read a few pages of a great book
[] Took photos of something beautiful
[] Started to learn a new skill
[] Laughed at something really funny

Today was fun
because.......................................
....
....

Happiness rating:

1 2 3 4 5 6 7 8 9 10

Day 28

I am grateful for:

1..
....

2..
....

3..
....

Today I:

[] Did 15 minutes of exercise
[] Sat quietly and relaxed (meditation)
[] Was kind to someone.
How?..
[] Spent time in nature
[] Listened to my favourite song
[] Ate something healthy
[] Called a friend
[] Hugged someone
[] Completed an unfinished task. What was
    it?..
[] Started/worked on a hobby
[] Read a few pages of a great book
[] Took photos of something beautiful
[] Started to learn a new skill
[] Laughed at something really funny

Today was fun
because...
....
....

Happiness rating:

        1 2 3 4 5 6 7 8 9 10

Why exercise?

Exercise has all kinds of benefits for your body and mind, most of which appear to help us feel happier! Scientific studies have found that exercising causes the release of hormones called endorphins, which relax us and make us feel good. Exercise can reduce your stress and anxiety, and can help you make new friends. It will also give you an energy boost!

There's more...!

You may find yourself feeling more confident, creative, and resilient, sleeping better, remembering more, and doing more with your day. And don't forget: exercising outside comes with extra benefits, like fresh air and connecting with nature.

www.pursuit-of-happiness.com *'Exercise' (ND)*

Hint
To avoid exercise becoming boring ask a friend or family member to join you, or try something you've never tried before!

Day 29

I am grateful for:

1...
....

2...
....

3...
....

Today I:

[] Did 15 minutes of exercise
[] Sat quietly and relaxed (meditation)
[] Was kind to someone.
How?..
[] Spent time in nature
[] Listened to my favourite song
[] Ate something healthy
[] Called a friend
[] Hugged someone
[] Completed an unfinished task. What was
   it?......................................
[] Started/worked on a hobby
[] Read a few pages of a great book
[] Took photos of something beautiful
[] Started to learn a new skill
[] Laughed at something really funny

Today was fun
because.....................................
....
....

Happiness rating:

        1 2 3 4 5 6 7 8 9 10

43

Day 30

I am grateful for:

1..
....

2..
....

3..
....

Today I:

[] Did 15 minutes of exercise
[] Sat quietly and relaxed (meditation)
[] Was kind to someone.
How?..
[] Spent time in nature
[] Listened to my favourite song
[] Ate something healthy
[] Called a friend
[] Hugged someone
[] Completed an unfinished task. What was
   it?..
[] Started/worked on a hobby
[] Read a few pages of a great book
[] Took photos of something beautiful
[] Started to learn a new skill
[] Laughed at something really funny

Today was fun
because...
....
....

Happiness rating:

1 2 3 4 5 6 7 8 9 10

Day 31

I am grateful for:

1..
....

2..
....

3..
....

Today I:

[] Did 15 minutes of exercise
[] Sat quietly and relaxed (meditation)
[] Was kind to someone.
How?...
[] Spent time in nature
[] Listened to my favourite song
[] Ate something healthy
[] Called a friend
[] Hugged someone
[] Completed an unfinished task. What was
   it?.......................................
[] Started/worked on a hobby
[] Read a few pages of a great book
[] Took photos of something beautiful
[] Started to learn a new skill
[] Laughed at something really funny

Today was fun
because.......................................
....
....

Happiness rating:

        1 2 3 4 5 6 7 8 9 10

―――

Day 32

I am grateful for:
1...
....
2...
....
3...
....

Today I:

[] Did 15 minutes of exercise
[] Sat quietly and relaxed (meditation)
[] Was kind to someone.
How?...
[] Spent time in nature
[] Listened to my favourite song
[] Ate something healthy
[] Called a friend
[] Hugged someone
[] Completed an unfinished task. What was
    it?.......................................
[] Started/worked on a hobby
[] Read a few pages of a great book
[] Took photos of something beautiful
[] Started to learn a new skill
[] Laughed at something really funny

Today was fun
because..
....
....

Happiness rating:

        1 2 3 4 5 6 7 8 9 10

Day 33

I am grateful for:

1..
....

2..
....

3..
....

Today I:

[] Did 15 minutes of exercise
[] Sat quietly and relaxed (meditation)
[] Was kind to someone.
How?......................................
[] Spent time in nature
[] Listened to my favourite song
[] Ate something healthy
[] Called a friend
[] Hugged someone
[] Completed an unfinished task. What was
   it?....................................
[] Started/worked on a hobby
[] Read a few pages of a great book
[] Took photos of something beautiful
[] Started to learn a new skill
[] Laughed at something really funny

Today was fun
because...................................
....
....

Happiness rating:

        1 2 3 4 5 6 7 8 9 10

Day 34

I am grateful for:

1..
....

2..
....

3..
....

Today I:

[] Did 15 minutes of exercise
[] Sat quietly and relaxed (meditation)
[] Was kind to someone.
How?.......................................
[] Spent time in nature
[] Listened to my favourite song
[] Ate something healthy
[] Called a friend
[] Hugged someone
[] Completed an unfinished task. What was
   it?......................................
[] Started/worked on a hobby
[] Read a few pages of a great book
[] Took photos of something beautiful
[] Started to learn a new skill
[] Laughed at something really funny

Today was fun
because.....................................
....
....

Happiness rating:

1 2 3 4 5 6 7 8 9 10

Day 35

I am grateful for:

1...
....

2...
....

3...
....

Today I:

[] Did 15 minutes of exercise
[] Sat quietly and relaxed (meditation)
[] Was kind to someone.
How?..
[] Spent time in nature
[] Listened to my favourite song
[] Ate something healthy
[] Called a friend
[] Hugged someone
[] Completed an unfinished task. What was
    it?..
[] Started/worked on a hobby
[] Read a few pages of a great book
[] Took photos of something beautiful
[] Started to learn a new skill
[] Laughed at something really funny

Today was fun
because......................................
....
....

Happiness rating:

        1 2 3 4 5 6 7 8 9 10

Easy ways to get (at least) 15 minutes of exercise!

1. Go for a walk/run
2. Skip
3. Bounce on a trampoline
4. Run up and down your stairs
5. Go for a ride on your bike
6. Dance (have a kitchen disco!)
7. Basketball
8. Help someone in the garden (mum or dad or a neighbour)
9. Get your skates on (roller skating, or ice-skating)
10. Kick a football around the park
11. Go for a swim
12. Play tag
13. Hula hoop
14. Skateboard
15. Ride your scooter
16. Wii fit or Xbox Kinect
17. Yoga
18. Martial arts
19. Rock climbing
20. Climb a tree

Day 36

I am grateful for:

1..
....

2..
....

3..
....

Today I:

[] Did 15 minutes of exercise
[] Sat quietly and relaxed (meditation)
[] Was kind to someone.
How?..
[] Spent time in nature
[] Listened to my favourite song
[] Ate something healthy
[] Called a friend
[] Hugged someone
[] Completed an unfinished task. What was
    it?..
[] Started/worked on a hobby
[] Read a few pages of a great book
[] Took photos of something beautiful
[] Started to learn a new skill
[] Laughed at something really funny

Today was fun
because.......................................
....
....

Happiness rating:

         1 2 3 4 5 6 7 8 9 10

___

Day 37

I am grateful for:

1..
....

2..
....

3..
....

Today I:

[] Did 15 minutes of exercise
[] Sat quietly and relaxed (meditation)
[] Was kind to someone.
How?...
[] Spent time in nature
[] Listened to my favourite song
[] Ate something healthy
[] Called a friend
[] Hugged someone
[] Completed an unfinished task. What was
   it?.......................................
[] Started/worked on a hobby
[] Read a few pages of a great book
[] Took photos of something beautiful
[] Started to learn a new skill
[] Laughed at something really funny

Today was fun
because......................................
....
....

Happiness rating:

1 2 3 4 5 6 7 8 9 10

Day 38

I am grateful for:
1...
....
2...
....
3...
....

Today I:

[] Did 15 minutes of exercise
[] Sat quietly and relaxed (meditation)
[] Was kind to someone.
How?.......................................
[] Spent time in nature
[] Listened to my favourite song
[] Ate something healthy
[] Called a friend
[] Hugged someone
[] Completed an unfinished task. What was
   it?.....................................
[] Started/worked on a hobby
[] Read a few pages of a great book
[] Took photos of something beautiful
[] Started to learn a new skill
[] Laughed at something really funny

Today was fun
because....................................
....
....

Happiness rating:

        1 2 3 4 5 6 7 8 9 10

Day 39

I am grateful for:

1..
....

2..
....

3..
....

Today I:

[] Did 15 minutes of exercise
[] Sat quietly and relaxed (meditation)
[] Was kind to someone.
How?...
[] Spent time in nature
[] Listened to my favourite song
[] Ate something healthy
[] Called a friend
[] Hugged someone
[] Completed an unfinished task. What was
   it?..
[] Started/worked on a hobby
[] Read a few pages of a great book
[] Took photos of something beautiful
[] Started to learn a new skill
[] Laughed at something really funny

Today was fun
because......................................
....
....

Happiness rating:

        1 2 3 4 5 6 7 8 9 10

Day 40

I am grateful for:

1..
....

2..
....

3..
....

Today I:

[] Did 15 minutes of exercise
[] Sat quietly and relaxed (meditation)
[] Was kind to someone.
How?......................................
[] Spent time in nature
[] Listened to my favourite song
[] Ate something healthy
[] Called a friend
[] Hugged someone
[] Completed an unfinished task. What was
   it?....................................
[] Started/worked on a hobby
[] Read a few pages of a great book
[] Took photos of something beautiful
[] Started to learn a new skill
[] Laughed at something really funny

Today was fun
because....................................
....
....

Happiness rating:

        1 2 3 4 5 6 7 8 9 10

Day 41

I am grateful for:

1...
....

2...
....

3...
....

Today I:

[] Did 15 minutes of exercise
[] Sat quietly and relaxed (meditation)
[] Was kind to someone.
How?...
[] Spent time in nature
[] Listened to my favourite song
[] Ate something healthy
[] Called a friend
[] Hugged someone
[] Completed an unfinished task. What was
   it?.......................................
[] Started/worked on a hobby
[] Read a few pages of a great book
[] Took photos of something beautiful
[] Started to learn a new skill
[] Laughed at something really funny

Today was fun
because.......................................
....
....

Happiness rating:

    1 2 3 4 5 6 7 8 9 10

Day 42

I am grateful for:

1...
....

2...
....

3...
....

Today I:

[] Did 15 minutes of exercise
[] Sat quietly and relaxed (meditation)
[] Was kind to someone.
How?...
[] Spent time in nature
[] Listened to my favourite song
[] Ate something healthy
[] Called a friend
[] Hugged someone
[] Completed an unfinished task. What was
   it?.......................................
[] Started/worked on a hobby
[] Read a few pages of a great book
[] Took photos of something beautiful
[] Started to learn a new skill
[] Laughed at something really funny

Today was fun
because.......................................
....
....

Happiness rating:

1   2   3   4   5   6   7   8   9   10

You can
be
WHATEVER
you want
to be!

Day 43

I am grateful for:
1..
....

2..
....

3..
....

Today I:

[] Did 15 minutes of exercise
[] Sat quietly and relaxed (meditation)
[] Was kind to someone.
How?..
[] Spent time in nature
[] Listened to my favourite song
[] Ate something healthy
[] Called a friend
[] Hugged someone
[] Completed an unfinished task. What was
   it?.......................................
[] Started/worked on a hobby
[] Read a few pages of a great book
[] Took photos of something beautiful
[] Started to learn a new skill
[] Laughed at something really funny

Today was fun
because.....................................
....
....

Happiness rating:

   1 2 3 4 5 6 7 8 9 10

Day 44

I am grateful for:

1..
....

2..
....

3..
....

Today I:

[] Did 15 minutes of exercise
[] Sat quietly and relaxed (meditation)
[] Was kind to someone.
How?......................................
[] Spent time in nature
[] Listened to my favourite song
[] Ate something healthy
[] Called a friend
[] Hugged someone
[] Completed an unfinished task. What was
   it?....................................
[] Started/worked on a hobby
[] Read a few pages of a great book
[] Took photos of something beautiful
[] Started to learn a new skill
[] Laughed at something really funny

Today was fun
because...................................
....
....

Happiness rating:

1 2 3 4 5 6 7 8 9 10

Day 45

I am grateful for:
1...
....

2...
....

3...
....

Today I:

[] Did 15 minutes of exercise
[] Sat quietly and relaxed (meditation)
[] Was kind to someone.
How?...
[] Spent time in nature
[] Listened to my favourite song
[] Ate something healthy
[] Called a friend
[] Hugged someone
[] Completed an unfinished task. What was
   it?.......................................
[] Started/worked on a hobby
[] Read a few pages of a great book
[] Took photos of something beautiful
[] Started to learn a new skill
[] Laughed at something really funny

Today was fun
because.......................................
....
....

Happiness rating:

        1 2 3 4 5 6 7 8 9 10

61

Day 46

I am grateful for:

1...

....

2...

....

3...

....

Today I:

[] Did 15 minutes of exercise
[] Sat quietly and relaxed (meditation)
[] Was kind to someone.
How?.......................................
[] Spent time in nature
[] Listened to my favourite song
[] Ate something healthy
[] Called a friend
[] Hugged someone
[] Completed an unfinished task. What was
   it?.....................................
[] Started/worked on a hobby
[] Read a few pages of a great book
[] Took photos of something beautiful
[] Started to learn a new skill
[] Laughed at something really funny

Today was fun
because....................................
....
....

Happiness rating:

1 2 3 4 5 6 7 8 9 10

Day 47

I am grateful for:

1..
....

2..
....

3..
....

Today I:

[] Did 15 minutes of exercise
[] Sat quietly and relaxed (meditation)
[] Was kind to someone.
How?.......................................
[] Spent time in nature
[] Listened to my favourite song
[] Ate something healthy
[] Called a friend
[] Hugged someone
[] Completed an unfinished task. What was
    it?....................................
[] Started/worked on a hobby
[] Read a few pages of a great book
[] Took photos of something beautiful
[] Started to learn a new skill
[] Laughed at something really funny

Today was fun
because....................................
....
....

Happiness rating:

        1 2 3 4 5 6 7 8 9 10

Day 48

I am grateful for:

1..
....
2..
....
3..
....

Today I:

[] Did 15 minutes of exercise
[] Sat quietly and relaxed (meditation)
[] Was kind to someone.
How?......................................
[] Spent time in nature
[] Listened to my favourite song
[] Ate something healthy
[] Called a friend
[] Hugged someone
[] Completed an unfinished task. What was
    it?......................................
[] Started/worked on a hobby
[] Read a few pages of a great book
[] Took photos of something beautiful
[] Started to learn a new skill
[] Laughed at something really funny

Today was fun
because..................................
....
....

Happiness rating:

     1 2 3 4 5 6 7 8 9 10

Day 49

I am grateful for:

1...
....

2...
....

3...
....

Today I:

[] Did 15 minutes of exercise
[] Sat quietly and relaxed (meditation)
[] Was kind to someone.
How?..
[] Spent time in nature
[] Listened to my favourite song
[] Ate something healthy
[] Called a friend
[] Hugged someone
[] Completed an unfinished task. What was
   it?...
[] Started/worked on a hobby
[] Read a few pages of a great book
[] Took photos of something beautiful
[] Started to learn a new skill
[] Laughed at something really funny

Today was fun
because...
....
....

Happiness rating:

        1 2 3 4 5 6 7 8 9 10

Self-care, self-talk, and self-awareness

Taking care of yourself in simple ways like brushing your teeth and hair, eating healthy food (most of the time anyway), wearing clean clothes, exercising, and generally taking care of your physical self, will help to start your day in a positive way, as well as help to build your self-esteem and confidence.

Your posture, or the way you hold yourself, can also impact your happiness. Are you standing up tall? Is your head up? Are you smiling? Doing these simple things with your body can make your brain think you're happy!

Tony Robbins *(2001), Unlimited Power*

The things you say to yourself throughout your day are also extremely important.

Are you being kind to yourself?
Would you want other people to speak to you the way you speak to yourself?

Are you noticing what's right?
Or what's wrong?
Are you anticipating the best? Or worst?

Checking in on your self-talk, and choosing to think positively about yourself and your day is a powerful way to be happier every day.

Hint
Help your own self-talk by speaking kindly to, and about, your friends!

Day 50

I am grateful for:

1...
....

2...
....

3...
....

Today I:

[] Did 15 minutes of exercise
[] Sat quietly and relaxed (meditation)
[] Was kind to someone.
How?...
[] Spent time in nature
[] Listened to my favourite song
[] Ate something healthy
[] Called a friend
[] Hugged someone
[] Completed an unfinished task. What was
    it?..
[] Started/worked on a hobby
[] Read a few pages of a great book
[] Took photos of something beautiful
[] Started to learn a new skill
[] Laughed at something really funny

Today was fun
because..
....
....

Happiness rating:

        1 2 3 4 5 6 7 8 9 10

———

Day 51

I am grateful for:

1..
....

2..
....

3..
....

Today I:

[] Did 15 minutes of exercise
[] Sat quietly and relaxed (meditation)
[] Was kind to someone.
How?...
[] Spent time in nature
[] Listened to my favourite song
[] Ate something healthy
[] Called a friend
[] Hugged someone
[] Completed an unfinished task. What was
    it?.......................................
[] Started/worked on a hobby
[] Read a few pages of a great book
[] Took photos of something beautiful
[] Started to learn a new skill
[] Laughed at something really funny

Today was fun
because...................................
....
....

Happiness rating:

    1 2 3 4 5 6 7 8 9 10

68

Day 52

I am grateful for:

1...
....

2...
....

3...
....

Today I:

[] Did 15 minutes of exercise
[] Sat quietly and relaxed (meditation)
[] Was kind to someone.
How?.......................................
[] Spent time in nature
[] Listened to my favourite song
[] Ate something healthy
[] Called a friend
[] Hugged someone
[] Completed an unfinished task. What was
    it?.....................................
[] Started/worked on a hobby
[] Read a few pages of a great book
[] Took photos of something beautiful
[] Started to learn a new skill
[] Laughed at something really funny

Today was fun
because....................................
....
....

Happiness rating:

        1 2 3 4 5 6 7 8 9 10

69

Day 53

I am grateful for:

1..

....

2..

....

3..

....

Today I:

[] Did 15 minutes of exercise
[] Sat quietly and relaxed (meditation)
[] Was kind to someone.
How?......................................
[] Spent time in nature
[] Listened to my favourite song
[] Ate something healthy
[] Called a friend
[] Hugged someone
[] Completed an unfinished task. What was
    it?......................................
[] Started/worked on a hobby
[] Read a few pages of a great book
[] Took photos of something beautiful
[] Started to learn a new skill
[] Laughed at something really funny

Today was fun
because......................................

....

....

Happiness rating:

1 2 3 4 5 6 7 8 9 10

Day 54

I am grateful for:

1...
....

2...
....

3...
....

Today I:

[] Did 15 minutes of exercise
[] Sat quietly and relaxed (meditation)
[] Was kind to someone.
How?....................................
[] Spent time in nature
[] Listened to my favourite song
[] Ate something healthy
[] Called a friend
[] Hugged someone
[] Completed an unfinished task. What was
   it?....................................
[] Started/worked on a hobby
[] Read a few pages of a great book
[] Took photos of something beautiful
[] Started to learn a new skill
[] Laughed at something really funny

Today was fun
because....................................
....
....

Happiness rating:

1 2 3 4 5 6 7 8 9 10

Day 55

I am grateful for:

1..
....

2..
....

3..
....

Today I:

[] Did 15 minutes of exercise
[] Sat quietly and relaxed (meditation)
[] Was kind to someone.
How?..
[] Spent time in nature
[] Listened to my favourite song
[] Ate something healthy
[] Called a friend
[] Hugged someone
[] Completed an unfinished task. What was
    it?..
[] Started/worked on a hobby
[] Read a few pages of a great book
[] Took photos of something beautiful
[] Started to learn a new skill
[] Laughed at something really funny

Today was fun
because.......................................
....
....

Happiness rating:

        1 2 3 4 5 6 7 8 9 10

Day 56

I am grateful for:

1..
....

2..
....

3..
....

Today I:

[] Did 15 minutes of exercise
[] Sat quietly and relaxed (meditation)
[] Was kind to someone.
How?...
[] Spent time in nature
[] Listened to my favourite song
[] Ate something healthy
[] Called a friend
[] Hugged someone
[] Completed an unfinished task. What was
   it?.......................................
[] Started/worked on a hobby
[] Read a few pages of a great book
[] Took photos of something beautiful
[] Started to learn a new skill
[] Laughed at something really funny

Today was fun
because......................................
....
....

Happiness rating:

        1 2 3 4 5 6 7 8 9 10

Check your progress

How are you?
Are you feeling happier? (I hope so!)
Are you feeling anything else? (Like more energetic, healthier, or closer to people...?)

Progress, or moving forward in any area of your life, is a major key to happiness. Simply put, we feel good when we're going somewhere or getting better at something.

Anything!

Truly! Anything you choose, from baton twirling, to mountain biking. (To being happy!)

Progress gives you a feeling of accomplishment, fulfilment and greater confidence. And having something to progress towards provides a focus and distraction from fear and worry.

So, check back on your goal! Are you moving towards it?

What can you do to keep progressing?

Tony Robbins (2012), *The one and only thing you need to be happy.*
training.tonyrobbins.com

Just keep going...

Day 57

I am grateful for:

1..
....

2..
....

3..
....

Today I:

[] Did 15 minutes of exercise
[] Sat quietly and relaxed (meditation)
[] Was kind to someone.
How?....................................
[] Spent time in nature
[] Listened to my favourite song
[] Ate something healthy
[] Called a friend
[] Hugged someone
[] Completed an unfinished task. What was
    it?...................................
[] Started/worked on a hobby
[] Read a few pages of a great book
[] Took photos of something beautiful
[] Started to learn a new skill
[] Laughed at something really funny

Today was fun
because.................................
....
....

Happiness rating:

1 2 3 4 5 6 7 8 9 10

Day 58

I am grateful for:

1..
....

2..
....

3..
....

Today I:

[] Did 15 minutes of exercise
[] Sat quietly and relaxed (meditation)
[] Was kind to someone.
How?...
[] Spent time in nature
[] Listened to my favourite song
[] Ate something healthy
[] Called a friend
[] Hugged someone
[] Completed an unfinished task. What was
   it?..
[] Started/worked on a hobby
[] Read a few pages of a great book
[] Took photos of something beautiful
[] Started to learn a new skill
[] Laughed at something really funny

Today was fun
because......................................
....
....

Happiness rating:

1 2 3 4 5 6 7 8 9 10

Day 59

I am grateful for:

1...
....

2...
....

3...
....

Today I:

[] Did 15 minutes of exercise
[] Sat quietly and relaxed (meditation)
[] Was kind to someone.
How?..
[] Spent time in nature
[] Listened to my favourite song
[] Ate something healthy
[] Called a friend
[] Hugged someone
[] Completed an unfinished task. What was
   it?...
[] Started/worked on a hobby
[] Read a few pages of a great book
[] Took photos of something beautiful
[] Started to learn a new skill
[] Laughed at something really funny

Today was fun
because...
....
....

Happiness rating:

        1 2 3 4 5 6 7 8 9 10

Day 60

I am grateful for:

1...
....

2...
....

3...
....

Today I:

[] Did 15 minutes of exercise
[] Sat quietly and relaxed (meditation)
[] Was kind to someone.
How?.......................................
[] Spent time in nature
[] Listened to my favourite song
[] Ate something healthy
[] Called a friend
[] Hugged someone
[] Completed an unfinished task. What was
   it?.....................................
[] Started/worked on a hobby
[] Read a few pages of a great book
[] Took photos of something beautiful
[] Started to learn a new skill
[] Laughed at something really funny

Today was fun
because.....................................
....
....

Happiness rating:

        1 2 3 4 5 6 7 8 9 10

Day 61

I am grateful for:

1...
....

2...
....

3...
....

Today I:

[] Did 15 minutes of exercise
[] Sat quietly and relaxed (meditation)
[] Was kind to someone.
How?...
[] Spent time in nature
[] Listened to my favourite song
[] Ate something healthy
[] Called a friend
[] Hugged someone
[] Completed an unfinished task. What was
     it?..
[] Started/worked on a hobby
[] Read a few pages of a great book
[] Took photos of something beautiful
[] Started to learn a new skill
[] Laughed at something really funny

Today was fun
because..
....
....

Happiness rating:

        1 2 3 4 5 6 7 8 9 10

Day 62

I am grateful for:

1...
....

2...
....

3...
....

Today I:

[] Did 15 minutes of exercise
[] Sat quietly and relaxed (meditation)
[] Was kind to someone.
How?...
[] Spent time in nature
[] Listened to my favourite song
[] Ate something healthy
[] Called a friend
[] Hugged someone
[] Completed an unfinished task. What was
   it?...
[] Started/worked on a hobby
[] Read a few pages of a great book
[] Took photos of something beautiful
[] Started to learn a new skill
[] Laughed at something really funny

Today was fun
because...
....
....

Happiness rating:

1   2   3   4   5   6   7   8   9   10

Day 63

I am grateful for:

1..
....

2..
....

3..
....

Today I:

[] Did 15 minutes of exercise
[] Sat quietly and relaxed (meditation)
[] Was kind to someone.
How?..
[] Spent time in nature
[] Listened to my favourite song
[] Ate something healthy
[] Called a friend
[] Hugged someone
[] Completed an unfinished task. What was
   it?..
[] Started/worked on a hobby
[] Read a few pages of a great book
[] Took photos of something beautiful
[] Started to learn a new skill
[] Laughed at something really funny

Today was fun
because...
....
....

Happiness rating:

1   2   3   4   5   6   7   8   9   10

Meditation Matters

Meditation is 'the cultivation of a calm and positive state of mind'.

thebuddhistcentre.com

You can become more relaxed, healthy and happy by using simple techniques such as concentrating on your breathing, or focusing all your attention on one thing.

Meditation can relax you by reducing stress, anxiety and depression, while at the same time helping you develop concentration, positivity and calm. Meditation can also bring you closer to your friends and family by encouraging compassion, forgiveness and love.

Practising meditation can even help you in your education by reducing stress, improving your attention, and potentially boosting your exam scores.

It can even help you get over fights with your friends!

What's not to be happy about?

Ariana Marini *(ND)*,
choices.scholastic.com

Day 64

I am grateful for:
1..
....
2..
....
3..
....

Today I:

[] Did 15 minutes of exercise
[] Sat quietly and relaxed (meditation)
[] Was kind to someone.
How?..
[] Spent time in nature
[] Listened to my favourite song
[] Ate something healthy
[] Called a friend
[] Hugged someone
[] Completed an unfinished task. What was
   it?..
[] Started/worked on a hobby
[] Read a few pages of a great book
[] Took photos of something beautiful
[] Started to learn a new skill
[] Laughed at something really funny

Today was fun
because.......................................
....
....

Happiness rating:

          1 2 3 4 5 6 7 8 9 10

Day 65

I am grateful for:

1..
....

2..
....

3..
....

Today I:

[] Did 15 minutes of exercise
[] Sat quietly and relaxed (meditation)
[] Was kind to someone.
How?...
[] Spent time in nature
[] Listened to my favourite song
[] Ate something healthy
[] Called a friend
[] Hugged someone
[] Completed an unfinished task. What was
   it?...
[] Started/worked on a hobby
[] Read a few pages of a great book
[] Took photos of something beautiful
[] Started to learn a new skill
[] Laughed at something really funny

Today was fun
because..
....
....

Happiness rating:

       1 2 3 4 5 6 7 8 9 10

___

Day 66

I am grateful for:

1..
....

2..
....

3..
....

Today I:

[] Did 15 minutes of exercise
[] Sat quietly and relaxed (meditation)
[] Was kind to someone.
How?......................................
[] Spent time in nature
[] Listened to my favourite song
[] Ate something healthy
[] Called a friend
[] Hugged someone
[] Completed an unfinished task. What was
   it?......................................
[] Started/worked on a hobby
[] Read a few pages of a great book
[] Took photos of something beautiful
[] Started to learn a new skill
[] Laughed at something really funny

Today was fun
because......................................
....
....

Happiness rating:

        1 2 3 4 5 6 7 8 9 10

Day 67

I am grateful for:
1...
....
2...
....
3...
....

Today I:

[] Did 15 minutes of exercise
[] Sat quietly and relaxed (meditation)
[] Was kind to someone.
How?...
[] Spent time in nature
[] Listened to my favourite song
[] Ate something healthy
[] Called a friend
[] Hugged someone
[] Completed an unfinished task. What was
   it?...
[] Started/worked on a hobby
[] Read a few pages of a great book
[] Took photos of something beautiful
[] Started to learn a new skill
[] Laughed at something really funny

Today was fun
because..
....
....

Happiness rating:

        1 2 3 4 5 6 7 8 9 10

Day 68

I am grateful for:

1...
....

2...
....

3...
....

Today I:

[] Did 15 minutes of exercise
[] Sat quietly and relaxed (meditation)
[] Was kind to someone.
How?.......................................
[] Spent time in nature
[] Listened to my favourite song
[] Ate something healthy
[] Called a friend
[] Hugged someone
[] Completed an unfinished task. What was
    it?......................................
[] Started/worked on a hobby
[] Read a few pages of a great book
[] Took photos of something beautiful
[] Started to learn a new skill
[] Laughed at something really funny

Today was fun
because....................................
....
....

Happiness rating:

        1 2 3 4 5 6 7 8 9 10

Day 69

I am grateful for:

1...
....

2...
....

3...
....

Today I:

[] Did 15 minutes of exercise
[] Sat quietly and relaxed (meditation)
[] Was kind to someone.
How?...
[] Spent time in nature
[] Listened to my favourite song
[] Ate something healthy
[] Called a friend
[] Hugged someone
[] Completed an unfinished task. What was
   it?...
[] Started/worked on a hobby
[] Read a few pages of a great book
[] Took photos of something beautiful
[] Started to learn a new skill
[] Laughed at something really funny

Today was fun
because...
....
....

Happiness rating:

1 2 3 4 5 6 7 8 9 10

Day 70

I am grateful for:

1..
....

2..
....

3..
....

Today I:

[] Did 15 minutes of exercise
[] Sat quietly and relaxed (meditation)
[] Was kind to someone.
How?..
[] Spent time in nature
[] Listened to my favourite song
[] Ate something healthy
[] Called a friend
[] Hugged someone
[] Completed an unfinished task. What was
   it?..
[] Started/worked on a hobby
[] Read a few pages of a great book
[] Took photos of something beautiful
[] Started to learn a new skill
[] Laughed at something really funny

Today was fun
because..
....
....

Happiness rating:

        1 2 3 4 5 6 7 8 9 10

89

Ways to meditate

1. Breathe slowly, in for five seconds and out for five seconds. Sit comfortably and concentrate on each breath.

2. Close your eyes and listen to the sounds around you. Is it raining? Are birds chirping? Are there people laughing?

3. Notice your thoughts without judging them. Let them drift into your mind and out again.

4. Visualisation. Close your eyes and imagine! You could be doing your favourite thing, or something completely out of the ordinary. Your imagination is unlimited!

5. Be in the present moment. Notice the world around you exactly as it is... What can you see? How does it smell? Sound? What is the temperature? You can do this while doing anything!

6. Immerse yourself in something you enjoy: painting, colouring in, cooking, playing sport, walking in the woods, or craft. Even playing video games can be meditative if you are concentrating completely!

7. At bedtime, concentrate on relaxing different parts of your body, starting with your toes and slowly moving up to the top your head.

Hint
Don't worry whether you're right or wrong, meditation is personal; enjoy it!

90

Day 71

I am grateful for:

1...
....

2...
....

3...
....

Today I:

[] Did 15 minutes of exercise
[] Sat quietly and relaxed (meditation)
[] Was kind to someone.
How?...
[] Spent time in nature
[] Listened to my favourite song
[] Ate something healthy
[] Called a friend
[] Hugged someone
[] Completed an unfinished task. What was
   it?...
[] Started/worked on a hobby
[] Read a few pages of a great book
[] Took photos of something beautiful
[] Started to learn a new skill
[] Laughed at something really funny

Today was fun
because...
....
....

Happiness rating:

    1 2 3 4 5 6 7 8 9 10

Day 72

I am grateful for:

1...
....

2...
....

3...
....

Today I:

[] Did 15 minutes of exercise
[] Sat quietly and relaxed (meditation)
[] Was kind to someone.
How?...
[] Spent time in nature
[] Listened to my favourite song
[] Ate something healthy
[] Called a friend
[] Hugged someone
[] Completed an unfinished task. What was
   it?...
[] Started/worked on a hobby
[] Read a few pages of a great book
[] Took photos of something beautiful
[] Started to learn a new skill
[] Laughed at something really funny

Today was fun
because..
....
....

Happiness rating:

    1 2 3 4 5 6 7 8 9 10

Day 73

I am grateful for:

1..
....

2..
....

3..
....

Today I:

[] Did 15 minutes of exercise
[] Sat quietly and relaxed (meditation)
[] Was kind to someone.
How?..
[] Spent time in nature
[] Listened to my favourite song
[] Ate something healthy
[] Called a friend
[] Hugged someone
[] Completed an unfinished task. What was
   it?..
[] Started/worked on a hobby
[] Read a few pages of a great book
[] Took photos of something beautiful
[] Started to learn a new skill
[] Laughed at something really funny

Today was fun
because...
....
....

Happiness rating:

         1 2 3 4 5 6 7 8 9 10

Day 74

I am grateful for:

1..
....
2..
....
3..
....

Today I:

[] Did 15 minutes of exercise
[] Sat quietly and relaxed (meditation)
[] Was kind to someone.
How?..
[] Spent time in nature
[] Listened to my favourite song
[] Ate something healthy
[] Called a friend
[] Hugged someone
[] Completed an unfinished task. What was
   it?...
[] Started/worked on a hobby
[] Read a few pages of a great book
[] Took photos of something beautiful
[] Started to learn a new skill
[] Laughed at something really funny

Today was fun
because.......................................
....
....

Happiness rating:

1 2 3 4 5 6 7 8 9 10

Day 75

I am grateful for:
1..
....
2..
....
3..
....

Today I:

[] Did 15 minutes of exercise
[] Sat quietly and relaxed (meditation)
[] Was kind to someone.
How?..
[] Spent time in nature
[] Listened to my favourite song
[] Ate something healthy
[] Called a friend
[] Hugged someone
[] Completed an unfinished task. What was
   it?.......................................
[] Started/worked on a hobby
[] Read a few pages of a great book
[] Took photos of something beautiful
[] Started to learn a new skill
[] Laughed at something really funny

Today was fun
because......................................
....
....

Happiness rating:

        1 2 3 4 5 6 7 8 9 10

Day 76

I am grateful for:

1...
....

2...
....

3...
....

Today I:

[] Did 15 minutes of exercise
[] Sat quietly and relaxed (meditation)
[] Was kind to someone.
How?...
[] Spent time in nature
[] Listened to my favourite song
[] Ate something healthy
[] Called a friend
[] Hugged someone
[] Completed an unfinished task. What was
    it?.......................................
[] Started/worked on a hobby
[] Read a few pages of a great book
[] Took photos of something beautiful
[] Started to learn a new skill
[] Laughed at something really funny

Today was fun
because...
....
....

Happiness rating:

        1 2 3 4 5 6 7 8 9 10

Day 77

I am grateful for:

1..
....

2..
....

3..
....

Today I:

[] Did 15 minutes of exercise
[] Sat quietly and relaxed (meditation)
[] Was kind to someone.
How?..
[] Spent time in nature
[] Listened to my favourite song
[] Ate something healthy
[] Called a friend
[] Hugged someone
[] Completed an unfinished task. What was
   it?..
[] Started/worked on a hobby
[] Read a few pages of a great book
[] Took photos of something beautiful
[] Started to learn a new skill
[] Laughed at something really funny

Today was fun
because...
....
....

Happiness rating:

        1 2 3 4 5 6 7 8 9 10

Life is fun!

Day 78

I am grateful for:

1..
....

2..
....

3..
....

Today I:

[] Did 15 minutes of exercise
[] Sat quietly and relaxed (meditation)
[] Was kind to someone.
How?..
[] Spent time in nature
[] Listened to my favourite song
[] Ate something healthy
[] Called a friend
[] Hugged someone
[] Completed an unfinished task. What was
    it?..
[] Started/worked on a hobby
[] Read a few pages of a great book
[] Took photos of something beautiful
[] Started to learn a new skill
[] Laughed at something really funny

Today was fun
because..
....
....

Happiness rating:

        1 2 3 4 5 6 7 8 9 10

Day 79

I am grateful for:

1...
....

2...
....

3...
....

Today I:

[] Did 15 minutes of exercise
[] Sat quietly and relaxed (meditation)
[] Was kind to someone.
How?...
[] Spent time in nature
[] Listened to my favourite song
[] Ate something healthy
[] Called a friend
[] Hugged someone
[] Completed an unfinished task. What was
   it?..
[] Started/worked on a hobby
[] Read a few pages of a great book
[] Took photos of something beautiful
[] Started to learn a new skill
[] Laughed at something really funny

Today was fun
because...
....
....

Happiness rating:

         1 2 3 4 5 6 7 8 9 10

Day 80

I am grateful for:

1...
....

2...
....

3...
....

Today I:

[] Did 15 minutes of exercise
[] Sat quietly and relaxed (meditation)
[] Was kind to someone.
How?...
[] Spent time in nature
[] Listened to my favourite song
[] Ate something healthy
[] Called a friend
[] Hugged someone
[] Completed an unfinished task. What was
   it?..
[] Started/worked on a hobby
[] Read a few pages of a great book
[] Took photos of something beautiful
[] Started to learn a new skill
[] Laughed at something really funny

Today was fun
because..
....
....

Happiness rating:

       1 2 3 4 5 6 7 8 9 10

Day 81

I am grateful for:

1...
....

2...
....

3...
....

Today I:

[] Did 15 minutes of exercise
[] Sat quietly and relaxed (meditation)
[] Was kind to someone.
How?...
[] Spent time in nature
[] Listened to my favourite song
[] Ate something healthy
[] Called a friend
[] Hugged someone
[] Completed an unfinished task. What was
   it?.......................................
[] Started/worked on a hobby
[] Read a few pages of a great book
[] Took photos of something beautiful
[] Started to learn a new skill
[] Laughed at something really funny

Today was fun
because.......................................
....
....

Happiness rating:

    1 2 3 4 5 6 7 8 9 10

Day 82

I am grateful for:
1..
....
2..
....
3..
....

Today I:

[] Did 15 minutes of exercise
[] Sat quietly and relaxed (meditation)
[] Was kind to someone.
How?..
[] Spent time in nature
[] Listened to my favourite song
[] Ate something healthy
[] Called a friend
[] Hugged someone
[] Completed an unfinished task. What was
   it?..
[] Started/worked on a hobby
[] Read a few pages of a great book
[] Took photos of something beautiful
[] Started to learn a new skill
[] Laughed at something really funny

Today was fun
because.......................................
....
....

Happiness rating:

     1 2 3 4 5 6 7 8 9 10

———

Day 83

I am grateful for:

1..
....

2..
....

3..
....

Today I:

[] Did 15 minutes of exercise
[] Sat quietly and relaxed (meditation)
[] Was kind to someone.
How?..
[] Spent time in nature
[] Listened to my favourite song
[] Ate something healthy
[] Called a friend
[] Hugged someone
[] Completed an unfinished task. What was
   it?..
[] Started/worked on a hobby
[] Read a few pages of a great book
[] Took photos of something beautiful
[] Started to learn a new skill
[] Laughed at something really funny

Today was fun
because...................................
....
....

Happiness rating:

    1 2 3 4 5 6 7 8 9 10

Day 84

I am grateful for:
1...
....

2...
....

3...
....

Today I:

[] Did 15 minutes of exercise
[] Sat quietly and relaxed (meditation)
[] Was kind to someone.
How?.......................................
[] Spent time in nature
[] Listened to my favourite song
[] Ate something healthy
[] Called a friend
[] Hugged someone
[] Completed an unfinished task. What was
    it?....................................
[] Started/worked on a hobby
[] Read a few pages of a great book
[] Took photos of something beautiful
[] Started to learn a new skill
[] Laughed at something really funny

Today was fun
because....................................
....
....

Happiness rating:

        1 2 3 4 5 6 7 8 9 10

A story about you
Visualisation Exercise

Hint
Get your mum or dad to read this to you.

Close your eyes and imagine...

Imagine you are walking along a golden sandy beach. It is a warm day and the breeze blowing through your hair and against your face is the perfect temperature.
You feel relaxed.

As you walk you notice the cool sand under your feet.
You can hear the waves gently lapping against the shore, and the seagulls calling to each other.
You feel joy.

There are other sounds too. People laughing and having a great time.
You smile, happy that they are happy.

You feel content.

As you walk, you feel all the tension and worry leaving your body, and blowing away in the wind.

You feel free.

YOU FEEL HAPPY.

Hint
If you like meditation, check out
Smilingmind.com.au

Day 85

I am grateful for:
1...
....
2...
....
3...
....

Today I:

[] Did 15 minutes of exercise
[] Sat quietly and relaxed (meditation)
[] Was kind to someone.
How?...
[] Spent time in nature
[] Listened to my favourite song
[] Ate something healthy
[] Called a friend
[] Hugged someone
[] Completed an unfinished task. What was
    it?...
[] Started/worked on a hobby
[] Read a few pages of a great book
[] Took photos of something beautiful
[] Started to learn a new skill
[] Laughed at something really funny

Today was fun
because..
....
....

Happiness rating:

    1 2 3 4 5 6 7 8 9 10

Day 86

I am grateful for:

1..
....

2..
....

3..
....

Today I:

[] Did 15 minutes of exercise
[] Sat quietly and relaxed (meditation)
[] Was kind to someone.
How?.......................................
[] Spent time in nature
[] Listened to my favourite song
[] Ate something healthy
[] Called a friend
[] Hugged someone
[] Completed an unfinished task. What was
    it?.....................................
[] Started/worked on a hobby
[] Read a few pages of a great book
[] Took photos of something beautiful
[] Started to learn a new skill
[] Laughed at something really funny

Today was fun
because.....................................
....
....

Happiness rating:

       1 2 3 4 5 6 7 8 9 10

Day 87

I am grateful for:

1..
....

2..
....

3..
....

Today I:

[] Did 15 minutes of exercise
[] Sat quietly and relaxed (meditation)
[] Was kind to someone.
How?..
[] Spent time in nature
[] Listened to my favourite song
[] Ate something healthy
[] Called a friend
[] Hugged someone
[] Completed an unfinished task. What was
    it?..
[] Started/worked on a hobby
[] Read a few pages of a great book
[] Took photos of something beautiful
[] Started to learn a new skill
[] Laughed at something really funny

Today was fun
because.......................................
....
....

Happiness rating:

        1 2 3 4 5 6 7 8 9 10

Day 88

I am grateful for:

1..
....

2..
....

3..
....

Today I:

[] Did 15 minutes of exercise
[] Sat quietly and relaxed (meditation)
[] Was kind to someone.
How?......................................
[] Spent time in nature
[] Listened to my favourite song
[] Ate something healthy
[] Called a friend
[] Hugged someone
[] Completed an unfinished task. What was
   it?......................................
[] Started/worked on a hobby
[] Read a few pages of a great book
[] Took photos of something beautiful
[] Started to learn a new skill
[] Laughed at something really funny

Today was fun
because......................................
....
....

Happiness rating:

         1 2 3 4 5 6 7 8 9 10

Day 89

I am grateful for:

1..
....

2..
....

3..
....

Today I:

[] Did 15 minutes of exercise
[] Sat quietly and relaxed (meditation)
[] Was kind to someone.
How?......................................
[] Spent time in nature
[] Listened to my favourite song
[] Ate something healthy
[] Called a friend
[] Hugged someone
[] Completed an unfinished task. What was
    it?......................................
[] Started/worked on a hobby
[] Read a few pages of a great book
[] Took photos of something beautiful
[] Started to learn a new skill
[] Laughed at something really funny

Today was fun
because......................................
....
....

Happiness rating:

         1 2 3 4 5 6 7 8 9 10

Day 90

I am grateful for:

1..
....

2..
....

3..
....

Today I:

[] Did 15 minutes of exercise
[] Sat quietly and relaxed (meditation)
[] Was kind to someone.
How?......................................
[] Spent time in nature
[] Listened to my favourite song
[] Ate something healthy
[] Called a friend
[] Hugged someone
[] Completed an unfinished task. What was
   it?......................................
[] Started/worked on a hobby
[] Read a few pages of a great book
[] Took photos of something beautiful
[] Started to learn a new skill
[] Laughed at something really funny

Today was fun
because......................................
....
....

Happiness rating:

        1 2 3 4 5 6 7 8 9 10

Day 91

I am grateful for:

1..
....

2..
....

3..
....

Today I:

[] Did 15 minutes of exercise
[] Sat quietly and relaxed (meditation)
[] Was kind to someone.
How?......................................
[] Spent time in nature
[] Listened to my favourite song
[] Ate something healthy
[] Called a friend
[] Hugged someone
[] Completed an unfinished task. What was
    it?......................................
[] Started/worked on a hobby
[] Read a few pages of a great book
[] Took photos of something beautiful
[] Started to learn a new skill
[] Laughed at something really funny

Today was fun
because......................................
....
....

Happiness rating:

        1 2 3 4 5 6 7 8 9 10

Why be kind?

"For every action, there is an equal and opposite reaction."

Isaac Newton

How does Newton's 3rd Law of Physics relate to kindness?
That's easy! All the kindness you give comes back to you. Kindness towards someone is not only a gift to them, but also to you. Selflessly doing something for someone else takes your mind off yourself and your worries, AND increases the likelihood of others being kind to you. Giving can fill you with joy, happiness, and make you feel worthwhile.

It's important, in your acts of kindness, to aim to give more than you would ever expect in return. The weird thing is, the kindness will always be returned... but not necessarily always from the person you gave it to!

In short, you get what you give... So give as much as you can!

"How do we change
the world?
One single act of
random kindness at a
time."

Evan Almighty

Day 92

I am grateful for:

1...
....

2...
....

3...
....

Today I:

[] Did 15 minutes of exercise
[] Sat quietly and relaxed (meditation)
[] Was kind to someone.
How?..
[] Spent time in nature
[] Listened to my favourite song
[] Ate something healthy
[] Called a friend
[] Hugged someone
[] Completed an unfinished task. What was
   it?..
[] Started/worked on a hobby
[] Read a few pages of a great book
[] Took photos of something beautiful
[] Started to learn a new skill
[] Laughed at something really funny

Today was fun
because..
....
....

Happiness rating:

1 2 3 4 5 6 7 8 9 10

Day 93

I am grateful for:

1..
....

2..
....

3..
....

Today I:

[] Did 15 minutes of exercise
[] Sat quietly and relaxed (meditation)
[] Was kind to someone.
How?...
[] Spent time in nature
[] Listened to my favourite song
[] Ate something healthy
[] Called a friend
[] Hugged someone
[] Completed an unfinished task. What was
   it?...
[] Started/worked on a hobby
[] Read a few pages of a great book
[] Took photos of something beautiful
[] Started to learn a new skill
[] Laughed at something really funny

Today was fun
because...
....
....

Happiness rating:

1 2 3 4 5 6 7 8 9 10

Day 94

I am grateful for:

1...
....

2...
....

3...
....

Today I:

[] Did 15 minutes of exercise
[] Sat quietly and relaxed (meditation)
[] Was kind to someone.
How?.......................................
[] Spent time in nature
[] Listened to my favourite song
[] Ate something healthy
[] Called a friend
[] Hugged someone
[] Completed an unfinished task. What was
   it?.......................................
[] Started/worked on a hobby
[] Read a few pages of a great book
[] Took photos of something beautiful
[] Started to learn a new skill
[] Laughed at something really funny

Today was fun
because......................................
....
....

Happiness rating:

    1 2 3 4 5 6 7 8 9 10

Day 95

I am grateful for:

1...
....

2...
....

3...
....

Today I:

[] Did 15 minutes of exercise
[] Sat quietly and relaxed (meditation)
[] Was kind to someone.
How?.......................................
[] Spent time in nature
[] Listened to my favourite song
[] Ate something healthy
[] Called a friend
[] Hugged someone
[] Completed an unfinished task. What was
   it?.....................................
[] Started/worked on a hobby
[] Read a few pages of a great book
[] Took photos of something beautiful
[] Started to learn a new skill
[] Laughed at something really funny

Today was fun
because....................................
....
....

Happiness rating:

        1 2 3 4 5 6 7 8 9 10

Day 96

I am grateful for:

1..
....

2..
....

3..
....

Today I:

[] Did 15 minutes of exercise
[] Sat quietly and relaxed (meditation)
[] Was kind to someone.
How?...
[] Spent time in nature
[] Listened to my favourite song
[] Ate something healthy
[] Called a friend
[] Hugged someone
[] Completed an unfinished task. What was
   it?.......................................
[] Started/worked on a hobby
[] Read a few pages of a great book
[] Took photos of something beautiful
[] Started to learn a new skill
[] Laughed at something really funny

Today was fun
because.......................................
....
....

Happiness rating:

        1 2 3 4 5 6 7 8 9 10

Day 97

I am grateful for:

1..
....

2..
....

3..
....

Today I:

[] Did 15 minutes of exercise
[] Sat quietly and relaxed (meditation)
[] Was kind to someone.
How?...
[] Spent time in nature
[] Listened to my favourite song
[] Ate something healthy
[] Called a friend
[] Hugged someone
[] Completed an unfinished task. What was
    it?..
[] Started/worked on a hobby
[] Read a few pages of a great book
[] Took photos of something beautiful
[] Started to learn a new skill
[] Laughed at something really funny

Today was fun
because..
....
....

Happiness rating:

        1 2 3 4 5 6 7 8 9 10

Day 98

I am grateful for:

1..
....

2..
....

3..
....

Today I:

[] Did 15 minutes of exercise
[] Sat quietly and relaxed (meditation)
[] Was kind to someone.
How?...
[] Spent time in nature
[] Listened to my favourite song
[] Ate something healthy
[] Called a friend
[] Hugged someone
[] Completed an unfinished task. What was
    it?.......................................
[] Started/worked on a hobby
[] Read a few pages of a great book
[] Took photos of something beautiful
[] Started to learn a new skill
[] Laughed at something really funny

Today was fun
because......................................
....
....

Happiness rating:

1 2 3 4 5 6 7 8 9 10

Easy ways to be kind

1. Offer to make your mum or dad a cuppa.

2. Open the door for a friend.

3. Help carry your neighbour's shopping.

4. Help with the chores.

5. Smile!

6. Pay your friend a compliment.

7. Raise money for a good cause.

8. Bake something yummy for your family, friend, neighbour or a charity.

9. Help your brother or sister with their homework.

10. Make a new friend.

11. Volunteer for an organisation.

12. Pack up your old books, clothes or toys and donate them.

Hint
Can you think of any more ways you can be kind?

Day 99

I am grateful for:

1..
....

2..
....

3..
....

Today I:

[] Did 15 minutes of exercise
[] Sat quietly and relaxed (meditation)
[] Was kind to someone.
How?..
[] Spent time in nature
[] Listened to my favourite song
[] Ate something healthy
[] Called a friend
[] Hugged someone
[] Completed an unfinished task. What was
   it?..
[] Started/worked on a hobby
[] Read a few pages of a great book
[] Took photos of something beautiful
[] Started to learn a new skill
[] Laughed at something really funny

Today was fun
because......................................
....
....

Happiness rating:

  1 2 3 4 5 6 7 8 9 10

Day 100

I am grateful for:

1..
....

2..
....

3..
....

Today I:

[] Did 15 minutes of exercise
[] Sat quietly and relaxed (meditation)
[] Was kind to someone.
How?..
[] Spent time in nature
[] Listened to my favourite song
[] Ate something healthy
[] Called a friend
[] Hugged someone
[] Completed an unfinished task. What was
    it?......................................
[] Started/worked on a hobby
[] Read a few pages of a great book
[] Took photos of something beautiful
[] Started to learn a new skill
[] Laughed at something really funny

Today was fun
because.....................................
....
....

Happiness rating:

        1 2 3 4 5 6 7 8 9 10

Day 101

I am grateful for:
1..
....
2..
....
3..
....

Today I:

[] Did 15 minutes of exercise
[] Sat quietly and relaxed (meditation)
[] Was kind to someone.
How?.......................................
[] Spent time in nature
[] Listened to my favourite song
[] Ate something healthy
[] Called a friend
[] Hugged someone
[] Completed an unfinished task. What was
   it?......................................
[] Started/worked on a hobby
[] Read a few pages of a great book
[] Took photos of something beautiful
[] Started to learn a new skill
[] Laughed at something really funny

Today was fun
because.....................................
....
....

Happiness rating:

         1 2 3 4 5 6 7 8 9 10

Day 102

I am grateful for:

1..
....

2..
....

3..
....

Today I:

[] Did 15 minutes of exercise
[] Sat quietly and relaxed (meditation)
[] Was kind to someone.
How?......................................
[] Spent time in nature
[] Listened to my favourite song
[] Ate something healthy
[] Called a friend
[] Hugged someone
[] Completed an unfinished task. What was
   it?....................................
[] Started/worked on a hobby
[] Read a few pages of a great book
[] Took photos of something beautiful
[] Started to learn a new skill
[] Laughed at something really funny

Today was fun
because...................................
....
....

Happiness rating:

1 2 3 4 5 6 7 8 9 10

Day 103

I am grateful for:

1......................................
....

2......................................
....

3......................................
....

Today I:

[] Did 15 minutes of exercise
[] Sat quietly and relaxed (meditation)
[] Was kind to someone.
How?...................................
[] Spent time in nature
[] Listened to my favourite song
[] Ate something healthy
[] Called a friend
[] Hugged someone
[] Completed an unfinished task. What was
   it?..................................
[] Started/worked on a hobby
[] Read a few pages of a great book
[] Took photos of something beautiful
[] Started to learn a new skill
[] Laughed at something really funny

Today was fun
because................................
....
....

Happiness rating:

1 2 3 4 5 6 7 8 9 10

Day 104

I am grateful for:

1..
....

2..
....

3..
....

Today I:

[] Did 15 minutes of exercise
[] Sat quietly and relaxed (meditation)
[] Was kind to someone.
How?.......................................
[] Spent time in nature
[] Listened to my favourite song
[] Ate something healthy
[] Called a friend
[] Hugged someone
[] Completed an unfinished task. What was
   it?......................................
[] Started/worked on a hobby
[] Read a few pages of a great book
[] Took photos of something beautiful
[] Started to learn a new skill
[] Laughed at something really funny

Today was fun
because....................................
....
....

Happiness rating:

       1 2 3 4 5 6 7 8 9 10

Day 105

I am grateful for:

1..
....

2..
....

3..
....

Today I:

[] Did 15 minutes of exercise
[] Sat quietly and relaxed (meditation)
[] Was kind to someone.
How?.......................................
[] Spent time in nature
[] Listened to my favourite song
[] Ate something healthy
[] Called a friend
[] Hugged someone
[] Completed an unfinished task. What was
    it?......................................
[] Started/worked on a hobby
[] Read a few pages of a great book
[] Took photos of something beautiful
[] Started to learn a new skill
[] Laughed at something really funny

Today was fun
because.....................................
....
....

Happiness rating:

1 2 3 4 5 6 7 8 9 10

What to do when things go wrong

Not everything always goes to plan...
Sometimes we have to deal with stress, pain,
anger, fear, frustration, anxiety or
depression. Here are some hints to help in
those moments of stress.

Breathe, slowly in through your nose and out
through your mouth. This will help relax
your body and re-focus your mind. Try
imagining that you are breathing in positive
emotions and breathing out the negative
ones.

Move. This helps to use up all the energy
that builds up when you're stressed. Tensing
and relaxing parts of your body, like your
fists (squeezing a ball) or shoulders, can
help. Getting out and running around will
help burn the stress hormones **and** release
happy hormones into your body.

Think your way out of the stress. Think back
and figure out what started your anxious
feelings. Can you change the way you're
thinking about it to make it ok?

*"The greatest weapon against stress
is our ability to choose one
thought over another."*

William James

And afterwards...

Go back to **gratitude**. Even when you're feeling really bad, finding **SOMETHING** to be grateful for will help you to see your life in a more positive light.

Speak to someone. Briefly sharing your thoughts and feelings will help you feel less alone, and may help you find a solution. (Don't dwell on it for too long though.)

Own it. Take responsibility for your reaction... How could you react to the situation differently? How could you take control and empower yourself?

"Happiness can be found in even the darkest of times, if one only remembers to turn on the light."

J.K. Rowling, *Harry Potter and the Prisoner of Azkaban*

Hint
Raising your level of happiness will help you cope better when things aren't going to plan.

Day 106

I am grateful for:

1...
....

2...
....

3...
....

Today I:

[] Did 15 minutes of exercise
[] Sat quietly and relaxed (meditation)
[] Was kind to someone.
How?...
[] Spent time in nature
[] Listened to my favourite song
[] Ate something healthy
[] Called a friend
[] Hugged someone
[] Completed an unfinished task. What was
   it?...
[] Started/worked on a hobby
[] Read a few pages of a great book
[] Took photos of something beautiful
[] Started to learn a new skill
[] Laughed at something really funny

Today was fun
because..
....
....

Happiness rating:

1 2 3 4 5 6 7 8 9 10

Day 107

I am grateful for:

1..
....

2..
....

3..
....

Today I:

[] Did 15 minutes of exercise
[] Sat quietly and relaxed (meditation)
[] Was kind to someone.
How?...
[] Spent time in nature
[] Listened to my favourite song
[] Ate something healthy
[] Called a friend
[] Hugged someone
[] Completed an unfinished task. What was
   it?...
[] Started/worked on a hobby
[] Read a few pages of a great book
[] Took photos of something beautiful
[] Started to learn a new skill
[] Laughed at something really funny

Today was fun
because..
....
....

Happiness rating:

     1 2 3 4 5 6 7 8 9 10

Day 108

I am grateful for:

1..
....

2..
....

3..
....

Today I:

[] Did 15 minutes of exercise
[] Sat quietly and relaxed (meditation)
[] Was kind to someone.
How?..
[] Spent time in nature
[] Listened to my favourite song
[] Ate something healthy
[] Called a friend
[] Hugged someone
[] Completed an unfinished task. What was
   it?..
[] Started/worked on a hobby
[] Read a few pages of a great book
[] Took photos of something beautiful
[] Started to learn a new skill
[] Laughed at something really funny

Today was fun
because..
....
....

Happiness rating:

        1 2 3 4 5 6 7 8 9 10

Day 109

I am grateful for:

1..
....

2..
....

3..
....

Today I:

[] Did 15 minutes of exercise
[] Sat quietly and relaxed (meditation)
[] Was kind to someone.
How?.......................................
[] Spent time in nature
[] Listened to my favourite song
[] Ate something healthy
[] Called a friend
[] Hugged someone
[] Completed an unfinished task. What was
   it?......................................
[] Started/worked on a hobby
[] Read a few pages of a great book
[] Took photos of something beautiful
[] Started to learn a new skill
[] Laughed at something really funny

Today was fun
because.......................................
....
....

Happiness rating:

1 2 3 4 5 6 7 8 9 10

Day 110

I am grateful for:

1..
....

2..
....

3..
....

Today I:

[] Did 15 minutes of exercise
[] Sat quietly and relaxed (meditation)
[] Was kind to someone.
How?..
[] Spent time in nature
[] Listened to my favourite song
[] Ate something healthy
[] Called a friend
[] Hugged someone
[] Completed an unfinished task. What was
    it?..
[] Started/worked on a hobby
[] Read a few pages of a great book
[] Took photos of something beautiful
[] Started to learn a new skill
[] Laughed at something really funny

Today was fun
because..
....
....

Happiness rating:

     1 2 3 4 5 6 7 8 9 10

Day 111

I am grateful for:
1...
....
2...
....
3...
....

Today I:

[] Did 15 minutes of exercise
[] Sat quietly and relaxed (meditation)
[] Was kind to someone.
How?......................................
[] Spent time in nature
[] Listened to my favourite song
[] Ate something healthy
[] Called a friend
[] Hugged someone
[] Completed an unfinished task. What was
    it?......................................
[] Started/worked on a hobby
[] Read a few pages of a great book
[] Took photos of something beautiful
[] Started to learn a new skill
[] Laughed at something really funny

Today was fun
because......................................
....
....

Happiness rating:

    1 2 3 4 5 6 7 8 9 10

Day 112

I am grateful for:

1..
....

2..
....

3..
....

Today I:

[] Did 15 minutes of exercise
[] Sat quietly and relaxed (meditation)
[] Was kind to someone.
How?..
[] Spent time in nature
[] Listened to my favourite song
[] Ate something healthy
[] Called a friend
[] Hugged someone
[] Completed an unfinished task. What was
    it?.....................................
[] Started/worked on a hobby
[] Read a few pages of a great book
[] Took photos of something beautiful
[] Started to learn a new skill
[] Laughed at something really funny

Today was fun
because......................................
....
....

Happiness rating:

    1 2 3 4 5 6 7 8 9 10

"We must face tomorrow, whatever it may hold, with determination, joy and bravery."

Mr Magorium's Wonder Emporium

Day 113

I am grateful for:
1..
....
2..
....
3..
....

Today I:

[] Did 15 minutes of exercise
[] Sat quietly and relaxed (meditation)
[] Was kind to someone.
How?.......................................
[] Spent time in nature
[] Listened to my favourite song
[] Ate something healthy
[] Called a friend
[] Hugged someone
[] Completed an unfinished task. What was
    it?.....................................
[] Started/worked on a hobby
[] Read a few pages of a great book
[] Took photos of something beautiful
[] Started to learn a new skill
[] Laughed at something really funny

Today was fun
because....................................
....
....

Happiness rating:

        1 2 3 4 5 6 7 8 9 10

Day 114

I am grateful for:

1...
....

2...
....

3...
....

Today I:

[] Did 15 minutes of exercise
[] Sat quietly and relaxed (meditation)
[] Was kind to someone.
How?.......................................
[] Spent time in nature
[] Listened to my favourite song
[] Ate something healthy
[] Called a friend
[] Hugged someone
[] Completed an unfinished task. What was
   it?.....................................
[] Started/worked on a hobby
[] Read a few pages of a great book
[] Took photos of something beautiful
[] Started to learn a new skill
[] Laughed at something really funny

Today was fun
because....................................
....
....

Happiness rating:

     1 2 3 4 5 6 7 8 9 10

Day 115

I am grateful for:

1......................................
....

2......................................
....

3......................................
....

Today I:

[] Did 15 minutes of exercise
[] Sat quietly and relaxed (meditation)
[] Was kind to someone.
How?..................................
[] Spent time in nature
[] Listened to my favourite song
[] Ate something healthy
[] Called a friend
[] Hugged someone
[] Completed an unfinished task. What was
   it?................................
[] Started/worked on a hobby
[] Read a few pages of a great book
[] Took photos of something beautiful
[] Started to learn a new skill
[] Laughed at something really funny

Today was fun
because................................
....
....

Happiness rating:

    1 2 3 4 5 6 7 8 9 10

Day 116

I am grateful for:

1..
....

2..
....

3..
....

Today I:

[] Did 15 minutes of exercise
[] Sat quietly and relaxed (meditation)
[] Was kind to someone.
How?......................................
[] Spent time in nature
[] Listened to my favourite song
[] Ate something healthy
[] Called a friend
[] Hugged someone
[] Completed an unfinished task. What was
   it?.....................................
[] Started/worked on a hobby
[] Read a few pages of a great book
[] Took photos of something beautiful
[] Started to learn a new skill
[] Laughed at something really funny

Today was fun
because...................................
....
....

Happiness rating:

1 2 3 4 5 6 7 8 9 10

Day 117

I am grateful for:

1..
....

2..
....

3..
....

Today I:

[] Did 15 minutes of exercise
[] Sat quietly and relaxed (meditation)
[] Was kind to someone.
How?...
[] Spent time in nature
[] Listened to my favourite song
[] Ate something healthy
[] Called a friend
[] Hugged someone
[] Completed an unfinished task. What was
    it?..
[] Started/worked on a hobby
[] Read a few pages of a great book
[] Took photos of something beautiful
[] Started to learn a new skill
[] Laughed at something really funny

Today was fun
because..
....
....

Happiness rating:

        1 2 3 4 5 6 7 8 9 10

Day 118

I am grateful for:

1...
....

2...
....

3...
....

Today I:

[] Did 15 minutes of exercise
[] Sat quietly and relaxed (meditation)
[] Was kind to someone.
How?.......................................
[] Spent time in nature
[] Listened to my favourite song
[] Ate something healthy
[] Called a friend
[] Hugged someone
[] Completed an unfinished task. What was
   it?..
[] Started/worked on a hobby
[] Read a few pages of a great book
[] Took photos of something beautiful
[] Started to learn a new skill
[] Laughed at something really funny

Today was fun
because..
....
....

Happiness rating:

       1   2   3   4   5   6   7   8   9   10

Day 119

I am grateful for:

1..
....

2..
....

3..
....

Today I:

[] Did 15 minutes of exercise
[] Sat quietly and relaxed (meditation)
[] Was kind to someone.
How?....................................
[] Spent time in nature
[] Listened to my favourite song
[] Ate something healthy
[] Called a friend
[] Hugged someone
[] Completed an unfinished task. What was
    it?..................................
[] Started/worked on a hobby
[] Read a few pages of a great book
[] Took photos of something beautiful
[] Started to learn a new skill
[] Laughed at something really funny

Today was fun
because.................................
....
....

Happiness rating:

1 2 3 4 5 6 7 8 9 10

Why nature?

Spending time in nature is great! Not only is it beneficial to your body, it also has positive effects on your mind! Physically, you feel better because your muscles relax, causing a reduction in stress. Sunlight boosts your immune system, and outdoor space gives you more opportunity to exercise, making you stronger, fitter and more energetic. You may also find you sleep better at night.

Department of Environmental Health (ND), *Immerse yourself in a forest for better health. www.dec.ny.gov*

Finding space outdoors in a park, woods or a garden gives you more opportunity to play 'how you like'! You get to make your own fun, like building, exploring, climbing trees, relaxing, running around... anything! This can help you become more creative, imaginative and inventive, which in turn can boost your self-confidence.
And also...
The sounds, smells and textures in nature can stimulate your senses, make you think more, and improve your concentration and memory.

American Society of Landscape Architects (ND), *Health Benefits of Nature. www.asla.org*

Hint
Just five minutes a day can benefit you. If it's hard to go outside, try putting up a poster of a forest or ocean in your room, or make nature the wallpaper on your technology devices!

Day 120

I am grateful for:

1..
....

2..
....

3..
....

Today I:

[] Did 15 minutes of exercise
[] Sat quietly and relaxed (meditation)
[] Was kind to someone.
How?..
[] Spent time in nature
[] Listened to my favourite song
[] Ate something healthy
[] Called a friend
[] Hugged someone
[] Completed an unfinished task. What was
    it?...
[] Started/worked on a hobby
[] Read a few pages of a great book
[] Took photos of something beautiful
[] Started to learn a new skill
[] Laughed at something really funny

Today was fun
because...
....
....

Happiness rating:

        1 2 3 4 5 6 7 8 9 10

Day 121

I am grateful for:

1..
....

2..
....

3..
....

Today I:

[] Did 15 minutes of exercise
[] Sat quietly and relaxed (meditation)
[] Was kind to someone.
How?......................................
[] Spent time in nature
[] Listened to my favourite song
[] Ate something healthy
[] Called a friend
[] Hugged someone
[] Completed an unfinished task. What was
   it?.....................................
[] Started/worked on a hobby
[] Read a few pages of a great book
[] Took photos of something beautiful
[] Started to learn a new skill
[] Laughed at something really funny

Today was fun
because...................................
....
....

Happiness rating:

　　　　1 2 3 4 5 6 7 8 9 10

Day 122

I am grateful for:

1...
....

2...
....

3...
....

Today I:

[] Did 15 minutes of exercise
[] Sat quietly and relaxed (meditation)
[] Was kind to someone.
How?...
[] Spent time in nature
[] Listened to my favourite song
[] Ate something healthy
[] Called a friend
[] Hugged someone
[] Completed an unfinished task. What was
   it?..
[] Started/worked on a hobby
[] Read a few pages of a great book
[] Took photos of something beautiful
[] Started to learn a new skill
[] Laughed at something really funny

Today was fun
because......................................
....
....

Happiness rating:

        1 2 3 4 5 6 7 8 9 10

Day 123

I am grateful for:

1..
....

2..
....

3..
....

Today I:

[] Did 15 minutes of exercise
[] Sat quietly and relaxed (meditation)
[] Was kind to someone.
How?...
[] Spent time in nature
[] Listened to my favourite song
[] Ate something healthy
[] Called a friend
[] Hugged someone
[] Completed an unfinished task. What was
   it?.......................................
[] Started/worked on a hobby
[] Read a few pages of a great book
[] Took photos of something beautiful
[] Started to learn a new skill
[] Laughed at something really funny

Today was fun
because......................................
....
....

Happiness rating:

        1 2 3 4 5 6 7 8 9 10

Day 124

I am grateful for:

1..
....

2..
....

3..
....

Today I:

[] Did 15 minutes of exercise
[] Sat quietly and relaxed (meditation)
[] Was kind to someone.
How?..
[] Spent time in nature
[] Listened to my favourite song
[] Ate something healthy
[] Called a friend
[] Hugged someone
[] Completed an unfinished task. What was
   it?......................................
[] Started/worked on a hobby
[] Read a few pages of a great book
[] Took photos of something beautiful
[] Started to learn a new skill
[] Laughed at something really funny

Today was fun
because......................................
....
....

Happiness rating:

    1 2 3 4 5 6 7 8 9 10

———
153

Day 125

I am grateful for:

1...
....

2...
....

3...
....

Today I:

[] Did 15 minutes of exercise
[] Sat quietly and relaxed (meditation)
[] Was kind to someone.
How?...
[] Spent time in nature
[] Listened to my favourite song
[] Ate something healthy
[] Called a friend
[] Hugged someone
[] Completed an unfinished task. What was
   it?...
[] Started/worked on a hobby
[] Read a few pages of a great book
[] Took photos of something beautiful
[] Started to learn a new skill
[] Laughed at something really funny

Today was fun
because..
....
....

Happiness rating:

        1 2 3 4 5 6 7 8 9 10

Day 126

I am grateful for:

1..
....

2..
....

3..
....

Today I:

[] Did 15 minutes of exercise
[] Sat quietly and relaxed (meditation)
[] Was kind to someone.
How?......................................
[] Spent time in nature
[] Listened to my favourite song
[] Ate something healthy
[] Called a friend
[] Hugged someone
[] Completed an unfinished task. What was
    it?......................................
[] Started/worked on a hobby
[] Read a few pages of a great book
[] Took photos of something beautiful
[] Started to learn a new skill
[] Laughed at something really funny

Today was fun
because......................................
....
....

Happiness rating:

        1 2 3 4 5 6 7 8 9 10

Ways to spend time in nature

1. Build a fort or cubby house.
2. Make some earth art.
3. Roll down a hill.
4. Play tag.
5. Build a fire and cook marshmallows. (Do this one safely!)
6. Take photos.
7. Take your shoes off and walk in the sand or grass.
8. Build an obstacle course.
9. Search for beetles.
10. Build a wildlife shelter (bug box or bird feeder).
11. Take your book/toys or iPod out into the garden.
12. Go for a walk with a dog (go with a friend if you don't have your own).
13. Climb a tree.
14. Pick some berries.
15. Lie in the sun (or shade).
16. Have a picnic.
17. Start a rock or shell collection.
18. Plant a tree/garden.
19. Go geocaching.
20. Go foraging for edible plants (make sure you do this with someone who knows about foraging!).
21. Go fishing.
22. Swim or paddle in a lake or river.
23. Sled down a snowy hill.
24. Play in the autumn leaves.
25. Explore the rock pools at the beach.
26. Fly a kite.

Hint
I'm sure you can think of more!

Day 127

I am grateful for:

1..
....

2..
....

3..
....

Today I:

[] Did 15 minutes of exercise
[] Sat quietly and relaxed (meditation)
[] Was kind to someone.
How?....................................
[] Spent time in nature
[] Listened to my favourite song
[] Ate something healthy
[] Called a friend
[] Hugged someone
[] Completed an unfinished task. What was
   it?..................................
[] Started/worked on a hobby
[] Read a few pages of a great book
[] Took photos of something beautiful
[] Started to learn a new skill
[] Laughed at something really funny

Today was fun
because.................................
....
....

Happiness rating:

        1 2 3 4 5 6 7 8 9 10

Day 128

I am grateful for:

1..
....

2..
....

3..
....

Today I:

[] Did 15 minutes of exercise
[] Sat quietly and relaxed (meditation)
[] Was kind to someone.
How?...
[] Spent time in nature
[] Listened to my favourite song
[] Ate something healthy
[] Called a friend
[] Hugged someone
[] Completed an unfinished task. What was
   it?..
[] Started/worked on a hobby
[] Read a few pages of a great book
[] Took photos of something beautiful
[] Started to learn a new skill
[] Laughed at something really funny

Today was fun
because..
....
....

Happiness rating:

1 2 3 4 5 6 7 8 9 10

Day 129

I am grateful for:

1...
....

2...
....

3...
....

Today I:

[] Did 15 minutes of exercise
[] Sat quietly and relaxed (meditation)
[] Was kind to someone.
How?...
[] Spent time in nature
[] Listened to my favourite song
[] Ate something healthy
[] Called a friend
[] Hugged someone
[] Completed an unfinished task. What was
   it?..
[] Started/worked on a hobby
[] Read a few pages of a great book
[] Took photos of something beautiful
[] Started to learn a new skill
[] Laughed at something really funny

Today was fun
because.......................................
....
....

Happiness rating:

       1 2 3 4 5 6 7 8 9 10

Day 130

I am grateful for:

1..
....

2..
....

3..
....

Today I:

[] Did 15 minutes of exercise
[] Sat quietly and relaxed (meditation)
[] Was kind to someone.
How?......................................
[] Spent time in nature
[] Listened to my favourite song
[] Ate something healthy
[] Called a friend
[] Hugged someone
[] Completed an unfinished task. What was
   it?......................................
[] Started/worked on a hobby
[] Read a few pages of a great book
[] Took photos of something beautiful
[] Started to learn a new skill
[] Laughed at something really funny

Today was fun
because......................................
....
....

Happiness rating:

1   2   3   4   5   6   7   8   9   10

Day 131

I am grateful for:

1...
....

2...
....

3...
....

Today I:

[] Did 15 minutes of exercise
[] Sat quietly and relaxed (meditation)
[] Was kind to someone.
How?...
[] Spent time in nature
[] Listened to my favourite song
[] Ate something healthy
[] Called a friend
[] Hugged someone
[] Completed an unfinished task. What was
    it?..
[] Started/worked on a hobby
[] Read a few pages of a great book
[] Took photos of something beautiful
[] Started to learn a new skill
[] Laughed at something really funny

Today was fun
because...
....
....

Happiness rating:

         1 2 3 4 5 6 7 8 9 10

Day 132

I am grateful for:

1..
....

2..
....

3..
....

Today I:

[] Did 15 minutes of exercise
[] Sat quietly and relaxed (meditation)
[] Was kind to someone.
How?..
[] Spent time in nature
[] Listened to my favourite song
[] Ate something healthy
[] Called a friend
[] Hugged someone
[] Completed an unfinished task. What was
   it?...
[] Started/worked on a hobby
[] Read a few pages of a great book
[] Took photos of something beautiful
[] Started to learn a new skill
[] Laughed at something really funny

Today was fun
because.......................................
....
....

Happiness rating:

        1 2 3 4 5 6 7 8 9 10

Day 133

I am grateful for:

1...
....

2...
....

3...
....

Today I:

[] Did 15 minutes of exercise
[] Sat quietly and relaxed (meditation)
[] Was kind to someone.
How?...
[] Spent time in nature
[] Listened to my favourite song
[] Ate something healthy
[] Called a friend
[] Hugged someone
[] Completed an unfinished task. What was
    it?.......................................
[] Started/worked on a hobby
[] Read a few pages of a great book
[] Took photos of something beautiful
[] Started to learn a new skill
[] Laughed at something really funny

Today was fun
because.......................................
....
....

Happiness rating:

        1 2 3 4 5 6 7 8 9 10

Music and happiness

Music makes us happy, this is no secret. I bet you know exactly what your favourite music is, and how it makes you feel. Music that moves you, makes you feel like singing at the top of your voice, or dancing around your house (happy music), has been shown to cause the release of 'happy hormones'(just like exercise). It also turns out that if you play a song thinking to yourself, "This will make me feel better", then the positive effect is even greater.

Suzanne Boothby (2013), *How Music Affects our Moods.* healthline.com

But it doesn't stop there. Music that has a sadder feel to it, and deals with deeper emotional issues, has the ability to help you feel happier too. (I know it sounds strange!) This is because it can help you identify and label potentially difficult emotions. It's also a great way to vent those negative emotions.

Jae Allen (2013), *How does Music Affect Teenagers' Emotions?* livestrong.com

Music can also bring you closer to other people and help you make new friends, by creating a sense of community around being fans together.

Whether you are playing your favourite tune, hanging out with your friends, going to a concert, or writing and playing your own, music is a gift, so enjoy!

———

Day 134

I am grateful for:

1...
....

2...
....

3...
....

Today I:

[] Did 15 minutes of exercise
[] Sat quietly and relaxed (meditation)
[] Was kind to someone.
How?...
[] Spent time in nature
[] Listened to my favourite song
[] Ate something healthy
[] Called a friend
[] Hugged someone
[] Completed an unfinished task. What was
   it?..
[] Started/worked on a hobby
[] Read a few pages of a great book
[] Took photos of something beautiful
[] Started to learn a new skill
[] Laughed at something really funny

Today was fun
because..
....
....

Happiness rating:

      1 2 3 4 5 6 7 8 9 10

Day 135

I am grateful for:

1..
....
2..
....
3..
....

Today I:

[] Did 15 minutes of exercise
[] Sat quietly and relaxed (meditation)
[] Was kind to someone.
How?..
[] Spent time in nature
[] Listened to my favourite song
[] Ate something healthy
[] Called a friend
[] Hugged someone
[] Completed an unfinished task. What was
   it?......................................
[] Started/worked on a hobby
[] Read a few pages of a great book
[] Took photos of something beautiful
[] Started to learn a new skill
[] Laughed at something really funny

Today was fun
because.....................................
....
....

Happiness rating:

1 2 3 4 5 6 7 8 9 10

Day 136

I am grateful for:

1..
....

2..
....

3..
....

Today I:

[] Did 15 minutes of exercise
[] Sat quietly and relaxed (meditation)
[] Was kind to someone.
How?....................................
[] Spent time in nature
[] Listened to my favourite song
[] Ate something healthy
[] Called a friend
[] Hugged someone
[] Completed an unfinished task. What was
   it?....................................
[] Started/worked on a hobby
[] Read a few pages of a great book
[] Took photos of something beautiful
[] Started to learn a new skill
[] Laughed at something really funny

Today was fun
because.................................
....
....

Happiness rating:

　　　1　2　3　4　5　6　7　8　9　10

Day 137

I am grateful for:

1..

....

2..

....

3..

....

Today I:

[] Did 15 minutes of exercise
[] Sat quietly and relaxed (meditation)
[] Was kind to someone.
How?..
[] Spent time in nature
[] Listened to my favourite song
[] Ate something healthy
[] Called a friend
[] Hugged someone
[] Completed an unfinished task. What was
    it?..
[] Started/worked on a hobby
[] Read a few pages of a great book
[] Took photos of something beautiful
[] Started to learn a new skill
[] Laughed at something really funny

Today was fun
because..
....
....

Happiness rating:

1   2   3   4   5   6   7   8   9   10

Day 138

I am grateful for:

1..
....

2..
....

3..
....

Today I:

[] Did 15 minutes of exercise
[] Sat quietly and relaxed (meditation)
[] Was kind to someone.
How?...
[] Spent time in nature
[] Listened to my favourite song
[] Ate something healthy
[] Called a friend
[] Hugged someone
[] Completed an unfinished task. What was
    it?.......................................
[] Started/worked on a hobby
[] Read a few pages of a great book
[] Took photos of something beautiful
[] Started to learn a new skill
[] Laughed at something really funny

Today was fun
because.......................................
....
....

Happiness rating:

        1 2 3 4 5 6 7 8 9 10

Day 139

I am grateful for:

1..
....

2..
....

3..
....

Today I:

[] Did 15 minutes of exercise
[] Sat quietly and relaxed (meditation)
[] Was kind to someone.
How?...
[] Spent time in nature
[] Listened to my favourite song
[] Ate something healthy
[] Called a friend
[] Hugged someone
[] Completed an unfinished task. What was
   it?...
[] Started/worked on a hobby
[] Read a few pages of a great book
[] Took photos of something beautiful
[] Started to learn a new skill
[] Laughed at something really funny

Today was fun
because..
....
....

Happiness rating:

        1 2 3 4 5 6 7 8 9 10

Day 140

I am grateful for:

1..
....

2..
....

3..
....

Today I:

[] Did 15 minutes of exercise
[] Sat quietly and relaxed (meditation)
[] Was kind to someone.
How?..
[] Spent time in nature
[] Listened to my favourite song
[] Ate something healthy
[] Called a friend
[] Hugged someone
[] Completed an unfinished task. What was
    it?......................................
[] Started/worked on a hobby
[] Read a few pages of a great book
[] Took photos of something beautiful
[] Started to learn a new skill
[] Laughed at something really funny

Today was fun
because......................................
....
....

Happiness rating:

        1 2 3 4 5 6 7 8 9 10

"When words fail,
music speaks."

Hans Christian Anderson

"...Dance like
nobody is
watching..."

Suzanne Clark and Richard Leigh,
Come from the Heart

Day 141

I am grateful for:

1..
....

2..
....

3..
....

Today I:

[] Did 15 minutes of exercise
[] Sat quietly and relaxed (meditation)
[] Was kind to someone.
How?..
[] Spent time in nature
[] Listened to my favourite song
[] Ate something healthy
[] Called a friend
[] Hugged someone
[] Completed an unfinished task. What was
   it?..
[] Started/worked on a hobby
[] Read a few pages of a great book
[] Took photos of something beautiful
[] Started to learn a new skill
[] Laughed at something really funny

Today was fun
because..
....
....

Happiness rating:

        1 2 3 4 5 6 7 8 9 10

Day 142

I am grateful for:

1..
....

2..
....

3..
....

Today I:

[] Did 15 minutes of exercise
[] Sat quietly and relaxed (meditation)
[] Was kind to someone.
How?..
[] Spent time in nature
[] Listened to my favourite song
[] Ate something healthy
[] Called a friend
[] Hugged someone
[] Completed an unfinished task. What was
   it?..
[] Started/worked on a hobby
[] Read a few pages of a great book
[] Took photos of something beautiful
[] Started to learn a new skill
[] Laughed at something really funny

Today was fun
because.....................................
....
....

Happiness rating:

1 2 3 4 5 6 7 8 9 10

Day 143

I am grateful for:

1..
....

2..
....

3..
....

Today I:

[] Did 15 minutes of exercise
[] Sat quietly and relaxed (meditation)
[] Was kind to someone.
How?..
[] Spent time in nature
[] Listened to my favourite song
[] Ate something healthy
[] Called a friend
[] Hugged someone
[] Completed an unfinished task. What was
   it?..
[] Started/worked on a hobby
[] Read a few pages of a great book
[] Took photos of something beautiful
[] Started to learn a new skill
[] Laughed at something really funny

Today was fun
because..
....
....

Happiness rating:

    1　2　3　4　5　6　7　8　9　10

Day 144

I am grateful for:

1..
....

2..
....

3..
....

Today I:

[] Did 15 minutes of exercise
[] Sat quietly and relaxed (meditation)
[] Was kind to someone.
How?..
[] Spent time in nature
[] Listened to my favourite song
[] Ate something healthy
[] Called a friend
[] Hugged someone
[] Completed an unfinished task. What was
   it?..
[] Started/worked on a hobby
[] Read a few pages of a great book
[] Took photos of something beautiful
[] Started to learn a new skill
[] Laughed at something really funny

Today was fun
because.......................................
....
....

Happiness rating:

1 2 3 4 5 6 7 8 9 10

Day 145

I am grateful for:

1..
....

2..
....

3..
....

Today I:

[] Did 15 minutes of exercise
[] Sat quietly and relaxed (meditation)
[] Was kind to someone.
How?..
[] Spent time in nature
[] Listened to my favourite song
[] Ate something healthy
[] Called a friend
[] Hugged someone
[] Completed an unfinished task. What was
   it?..
[] Started/worked on a hobby
[] Read a few pages of a great book
[] Took photos of something beautiful
[] Started to learn a new skill
[] Laughed at something really funny

Today was fun
because.......................................
....
....

Happiness rating:

        1 2 3 4 5 6 7 8 9 10

Day 146

I am grateful for:

1...
....

2...
....

3...
....

Today I:

[] Did 15 minutes of exercise
[] Sat quietly and relaxed (meditation)
[] Was kind to someone.
How?.......................................
[] Spent time in nature
[] Listened to my favourite song
[] Ate something healthy
[] Called a friend
[] Hugged someone
[] Completed an unfinished task. What was
   it?.......................................
[] Started/worked on a hobby
[] Read a few pages of a great book
[] Took photos of something beautiful
[] Started to learn a new skill
[] Laughed at something really funny

Today was fun
because.......................................
....
....

Happiness rating:

        1 2 3 4 5 6 7 8 9 10

Day 147

I am grateful for:

1..
....

2..
....

3..
....

Today I:

[] Did 15 minutes of exercise
[] Sat quietly and relaxed (meditation)
[] Was kind to someone.
How?..
[] Spent time in nature
[] Listened to my favourite song
[] Ate something healthy
[] Called a friend
[] Hugged someone
[] Completed an unfinished task. What was
    it?......................................
[] Started/worked on a hobby
[] Read a few pages of a great book
[] Took photos of something beautiful
[] Started to learn a new skill
[] Laughed at something really funny

Today was fun
because......................................
....
....

Happiness rating:

        1 2 3 4 5 6 7 8 9 10

Moody Food

Food affects you... and me... and everyone.
Physically, the different nutrients
contained in food lead to hormonal and
physical changes in your body.
Take chocolate: substances in dark chocolate
have been shown to cause the release of
endorphins (those happy hormones again), as
well as reducing fatigue and irritability,
and potentially triggering feelings of
euphoria.
Foods such as fruit, vegetables and natural
yoghurt, as well as coffee and green tea,
have also been shown to increase happiness
and give a greater sense of well-being.
Cynthia Sass *(2015), 6 foods that make you happier.*
news.health.com

There is also an emotional side to eating.
It feels good, satisfies hunger, warms you
up, cools you down and can give you a sense
of fulfilment. We eat for comfort, based on
how we already feel about the food we're
eating.
These feelings come from what we're eating,
whom we're eating with, where we're eating,
and our past experiences.
There is nothing wrong with comfort eating:
a yummy hot chocolate on a cold day, popcorn
at the movies, or a bag of sweets shared
with a friend won't do any harm at all.
The key is to keep it in balance and enjoy
the experience!

Hint
If you are having strong negative feelings
about food and eating, or you're comfort
eating for negative reasons, speak to
someone and get some help.

Day 148

I am grateful for:

1..
....

2..
....

3..
....

Today I:

[] Did 15 minutes of exercise
[] Sat quietly and relaxed (meditation)
[] Was kind to someone.
How?..
[] Spent time in nature
[] Listened to my favourite song
[] Ate something healthy
[] Called a friend
[] Hugged someone
[] Completed an unfinished task. What was
   it?......................................
[] Started/worked on a hobby
[] Read a few pages of a great book
[] Took photos of something beautiful
[] Started to learn a new skill
[] Laughed at something really funny

Today was fun
because.....................................
....
....

Happiness rating:

1 2 3 4 5 6 7 8 9 10

Day 149

I am grateful for:

1...
....

2...
....

3...
....

Today I:

[] Did 15 minutes of exercise
[] Sat quietly and relaxed (meditation)
[] Was kind to someone.
How?.......................................
[] Spent time in nature
[] Listened to my favourite song
[] Ate something healthy
[] Called a friend
[] Hugged someone
[] Completed an unfinished task. What was
    it?......................................
[] Started/worked on a hobby
[] Read a few pages of a great book
[] Took photos of something beautiful
[] Started to learn a new skill
[] Laughed at something really funny

Today was fun
because.....................................
....
....

Happiness rating:

        1 2 3 4 5 6 7 8 9 10

Day 150

I am grateful for:

1..
....

2..
....

3..
....

Today I:

[] Did 15 minutes of exercise
[] Sat quietly and relaxed (meditation)
[] Was kind to someone.
How?...
[] Spent time in nature
[] Listened to my favourite song
[] Ate something healthy
[] Called a friend
[] Hugged someone
[] Completed an unfinished task. What was
   it?.......................................
[] Started/worked on a hobby
[] Read a few pages of a great book
[] Took photos of something beautiful
[] Started to learn a new skill
[] Laughed at something really funny

Today was fun
because......................................
....
....

Happiness rating:

        1 2 3 4 5 6 7 8 9 10

Day 151

I am grateful for:

1..
....

2..
....

3..
....

Today I:

[] Did 15 minutes of exercise
[] Sat quietly and relaxed (meditation)
[] Was kind to someone.
How?......................................
[] Spent time in nature
[] Listened to my favourite song
[] Ate something healthy
[] Called a friend
[] Hugged someone
[] Completed an unfinished task. What was
   it?......................................
[] Started/worked on a hobby
[] Read a few pages of a great book
[] Took photos of something beautiful
[] Started to learn a new skill
[] Laughed at something really funny

Today was fun
because......................................
....
....

Happiness rating:

1 2 3 4 5 6 7 8 9 10

Day 152

I am grateful for:

1...
....

2...
....

3...
....

Today I:

[] Did 15 minutes of exercise
[] Sat quietly and relaxed (meditation)
[] Was kind to someone.
How?.......................................
[] Spent time in nature
[] Listened to my favourite song
[] Ate something healthy
[] Called a friend
[] Hugged someone
[] Completed an unfinished task. What was
   it?.....................................
[] Started/worked on a hobby
[] Read a few pages of a great book
[] Took photos of something beautiful
[] Started to learn a new skill
[] Laughed at something really funny

Today was fun
because....................................
....
....

Happiness rating:

　　　1　2　3　4　5　6　7　8　9　10

Day 153

I am grateful for:

1..
....

2..
....

3..
....

Today I:

[] Did 15 minutes of exercise
[] Sat quietly and relaxed (meditation)
[] Was kind to someone.
How?..
[] Spent time in nature
[] Listened to my favourite song
[] Ate something healthy
[] Called a friend
[] Hugged someone
[] Completed an unfinished task. What was
    it?..
[] Started/worked on a hobby
[] Read a few pages of a great book
[] Took photos of something beautiful
[] Started to learn a new skill
[] Laughed at something really funny

Today was fun
because.....................................,...
....
....

Happiness rating:

1 2 3 4 5 6 7 8 9 10

Day 154

I am grateful for:

1..
....

2..
....

3..
....

Today I:

[] Did 15 minutes of exercise
[] Sat quietly and relaxed (meditation)
[] Was kind to someone.
How?..
[] Spent time in nature
[] Listened to my favourite song
[] Ate something healthy
[] Called a friend
[] Hugged someone
[] Completed an unfinished task. What was
    it?.....................................
[] Started/worked on a hobby
[] Read a few pages of a great book
[] Took photos of something beautiful
[] Started to learn a new skill
[] Laughed at something really funny

Today was fun
because.....................................
....
....

Happiness rating:

    1 2 3 4 5 6 7 8 9 10

Happy Snacks

Making your own food is a great way to boost your confidence and help you feel more empowered. These ideas are easy, but make sure you ask for help with the microwave, knives and stove if you need them.

1. Natural yoghurt with fresh fruit and honey. Chop the fruit, spoon it into a bowl with the yoghurt and honey, and eat!
2. Pita pocket pizzas. Spread a pita with passata, grated cheese and your choice of topping, like olives, peppers, ham and tomatoes. Bake. Eat.
3. Hummus and veggies. Cut carrots, peppers and cucumbers into sticks, dip into the hummus and eat! (Crackers and cheese are also great with this.)
4. Tomato, mozzarella and basil salad. Slice and layer the three ingredients on a plate. Drizzle with olive oil. Eat.
5. Fruit skewers drizzled in chocolate. Cut any fruit you like into bite-sized pieces and thread onto a skewer. Melt some chocolate in the microwave and drizzle over. Eat.
6. Pancakes. Whisk together one mug of flour, one mug of milk and one egg in a bowl. Ladle small amounts into a hot frying pan with melted butter. Flip them when the bubbles start popping to cook the other side. Serve with anything! (Jam, honey, sugar and lemon, peanut butter, or even cheese, tomato and ham.)

Hint
Self-raising flour will give you fat fluffy pancakes, and plain flour will give you thin ones.

Day 155

I am grateful for:

1..
....

2..
....

3..
....

Today I:

[] Did 15 minutes of exercise
[] Sat quietly and relaxed (meditation)
[] Was kind to someone.
How?..
[] Spent time in nature
[] Listened to my favourite song
[] Ate something healthy
[] Called a friend
[] Hugged someone
[] Completed an unfinished task. What was
   it?..
[] Started/worked on a hobby
[] Read a few pages of a great book
[] Took photos of something beautiful
[] Started to learn a new skill
[] Laughed at something really funny

Today was fun
because.......................................
....
....

Happiness rating:

     1 2 3 4 5 6 7 8 9 10

Day 156

I am grateful for:

1...
....

2...
....

3...
....

Today I:

[] Did 15 minutes of exercise
[] Sat quietly and relaxed (meditation)
[] Was kind to someone.
How?..
[] Spent time in nature
[] Listened to my favourite song
[] Ate something healthy
[] Called a friend
[] Hugged someone
[] Completed an unfinished task. What was
   it?..
[] Started/worked on a hobby
[] Read a few pages of a great book
[] Took photos of something beautiful
[] Started to learn a new skill
[] Laughed at something really funny

Today was fun
because..
....
....

Happiness rating:

        1 2 3 4 5 6 7 8 9 10

Day 157

I am grateful for:

1...
....

2...
....

3...
....

Today I:

[] Did 15 minutes of exercise
[] Sat quietly and relaxed (meditation)
[] Was kind to someone.
How?...
[] Spent time in nature
[] Listened to my favourite song
[] Ate something healthy
[] Called a friend
[] Hugged someone
[] Completed an unfinished task. What was
    it?.......................................
[] Started/worked on a hobby
[] Read a few pages of a great book
[] Took photos of something beautiful
[] Started to learn a new skill
[] Laughed at something really funny

Today was fun
because.......................................
....
....

Happiness rating:

        1 2 3 4 5 6 7 8 9 10

Day 158

I am grateful for:

1...
....

2...
....

3...
....

Today I:

[] Did 15 minutes of exercise
[] Sat quietly and relaxed (meditation)
[] Was kind to someone.
How?......................................
[] Spent time in nature
[] Listened to my favourite song
[] Ate something healthy
[] Called a friend
[] Hugged someone
[] Completed an unfinished task. What was
    it?....................................
[] Started/worked on a hobby
[] Read a few pages of a great book
[] Took photos of something beautiful
[] Started to learn a new skill
[] Laughed at something really funny

Today was fun
because....................................
....
....

Happiness rating:

1 2 3 4 5 6 7 8 9 10

Day 159

I am grateful for:
1..
....

2..
....

3..
....

Today I:

[] Did 15 minutes of exercise
[] Sat quietly and relaxed (meditation)
[] Was kind to someone.
How?..
[] Spent time in nature
[] Listened to my favourite song
[] Ate something healthy
[] Called a friend
[] Hugged someone
[] Completed an unfinished task. What was
    it?..
[] Started/worked on a hobby
[] Read a few pages of a great book
[] Took photos of something beautiful
[] Started to learn a new skill
[] Laughed at something really funny

Today was fun
because..
....
....

Happiness rating:

        1 2 3 4 5 6 7 8 9 10

Day 160

I am grateful for:

1..
....

2..
....

3..
....

Today I:

[] Did 15 minutes of exercise
[] Sat quietly and relaxed (meditation)
[] Was kind to someone.
How?......................................
[] Spent time in nature
[] Listened to my favourite song
[] Ate something healthy
[] Called a friend
[] Hugged someone
[] Completed an unfinished task. What was
   it?......................................
[] Started/worked on a hobby
[] Read a few pages of a great book
[] Took photos of something beautiful
[] Started to learn a new skill
[] Laughed at something really funny

Today was fun
because......................................
....
....

Happiness rating:

1 2 3 4 5 6 7 8 9 10

Day 161

I am grateful for:

1..
....

2..
....

3..
....

Today I:

[] Did 15 minutes of exercise
[] Sat quietly and relaxed (meditation)
[] Was kind to someone.
How?.......................................
[] Spent time in nature
[] Listened to my favourite song
[] Ate something healthy
[] Called a friend
[] Hugged someone
[] Completed an unfinished task. What was
    it?....................................
[] Started/worked on a hobby
[] Read a few pages of a great book
[] Took photos of something beautiful
[] Started to learn a new skill
[] Laughed at something really funny

Today was fun
because.....................................
....
....

Happiness rating:

        1 2 3 4 5 6 7 8 9 10

"All you need is love.
But a little chocolate
now and then doesn't
hurt."

Charles Schulz, author of *Peanuts*

Day 162

I am grateful for:

1..
....

2..
....

3..
....

Today I:

[] Did 15 minutes of exercise
[] Sat quietly and relaxed (meditation)
[] Was kind to someone.
How?...
[] Spent time in nature
[] Listened to my favourite song
[] Ate something healthy
[] Called a friend
[] Hugged someone
[] Completed an unfinished task. What was
    it?.......................................
[] Started/worked on a hobby
[] Read a few pages of a great book
[] Took photos of something beautiful
[] Started to learn a new skill
[] Laughed at something really funny

Today was fun
because.......................................
....
....

Happiness rating:

    1 2 3 4 5 6 7 8 9 10

Day 163

I am grateful for:

1...
....

2...
....

3...
....

Today I:

[] Did 15 minutes of exercise
[] Sat quietly and relaxed (meditation)
[] Was kind to someone.
How?..
[] Spent time in nature
[] Listened to my favourite song
[] Ate something healthy
[] Called a friend
[] Hugged someone
[] Completed an unfinished task. What was
   it?..
[] Started/worked on a hobby
[] Read a few pages of a great book
[] Took photos of something beautiful
[] Started to learn a new skill
[] Laughed at something really funny

Today was fun
because..
....
....

Happiness rating:

        1 2 3 4 5 6 7 8 9 10

Day 164

I am grateful for:

1...
....

2...
....

3...
....

Today I:

[] Did 15 minutes of exercise
[] Sat quietly and relaxed (meditation)
[] Was kind to someone.
How?.......................................
[] Spent time in nature
[] Listened to my favourite song
[] Ate something healthy
[] Called a friend
[] Hugged someone
[] Completed an unfinished task. What was
    it?.....................................
[] Started/worked on a hobby
[] Read a few pages of a great book
[] Took photos of something beautiful
[] Started to learn a new skill
[] Laughed at something really funny

Today was fun
because.....................................
....
....

Happiness rating:

        1 2 3 4 5 6 7 8 9 10

Day 165

I am grateful for:

1..
....
2..
....
3..
....

Today I:

[] Did 15 minutes of exercise
[] Sat quietly and relaxed (meditation)
[] Was kind to someone.
How?..
[] Spent time in nature
[] Listened to my favourite song
[] Ate something healthy
[] Called a friend
[] Hugged someone
[] Completed an unfinished task. What was
   it?.......................................
[] Started/worked on a hobby
[] Read a few pages of a great book
[] Took photos of something beautiful
[] Started to learn a new skill
[] Laughed at something really funny

Today was fun
because......................................
....
....

Happiness rating:

1 2 3 4 5 6 7 8 9 10

Day 166

I am grateful for:
1..
....
2..
....
3..
....

Today I:

[] Did 15 minutes of exercise
[] Sat quietly and relaxed (meditation)
[] Was kind to someone.
How?..
[] Spent time in nature
[] Listened to my favourite song
[] Ate something healthy
[] Called a friend
[] Hugged someone
[] Completed an unfinished task. What was
    it?..
[] Started/worked on a hobby
[] Read a few pages of a great book
[] Took photos of something beautiful
[] Started to learn a new skill
[] Laughed at something really funny

Today was fun
because...
....
....

Happiness rating:

    1   2   3   4   5   6   7   8   9   10

Day 167

I am grateful for:

1...
....

2...
....

3...
....

Today I:

[] Did 15 minutes of exercise
[] Sat quietly and relaxed (meditation)
[] Was kind to someone.
How?...
[] Spent time in nature
[] Listened to my favourite song
[] Ate something healthy
[] Called a friend
[] Hugged someone
[] Completed an unfinished task. What was
   it?.......................................
[] Started/worked on a hobby
[] Read a few pages of a great book
[] Took photos of something beautiful
[] Started to learn a new skill
[] Laughed at something really funny

Today was fun
because......................................
....
....

Happiness rating:

      1 2 3 4 5 6 7 8 9 10

Day 168

I am grateful for:

1..
....

2..
....

3..
....

Today I:

[] Did 15 minutes of exercise
[] Sat quietly and relaxed (meditation)
[] Was kind to someone.
How?...
[] Spent time in nature
[] Listened to my favourite song
[] Ate something healthy
[] Called a friend
[] Hugged someone
[] Completed an unfinished task. What was
   it?.......................................
[] Started/worked on a hobby
[] Read a few pages of a great book
[] Took photos of something beautiful
[] Started to learn a new skill
[] Laughed at something really funny

Today was fun
because......................................
....
....

Happiness rating:

  1 2 3 4 5 6 7 8 9 10

It's Personal
The value of good relationships

When it comes to being happy, our close relationships really matter, and it is the quality (not quantity) of these relationships that can have a huge impact on our current and future happiness.
Feeling secure in your most important relationships, with your parents, siblings, and closest friends, makes you feel supported, worthwhile, accepted and loved for who you are.
Your wider community of friends gives you a sense of belonging and can help boost your confidence and self-esteem!
Different friends will come into your life at various times, and generally meet different needs, from bringing out your fun, competitive side on the sports field, to sharing your deepest secrets. Friends are the stars in your life, and whatever purpose they fulfil, your friendships require nurturing.
Being a good friend is just as important as having good friends, as it literally goes both ways. (Your friendship will make your friends happier too!) Sharing good times, supporting each other in hard times, talking and listening, and showing mutual respect are all building blocks for great friendships.
Hint Sadly, friendships gone wrong can be a source of unhappiness too, so if you are consistently feeling let down or unhappy, and can't work it out, it's also ok to let go.
10 keys to happier living - Family and Friends (ND)
www.actionforhappiness.org

Day 169

I am grateful for:

1...
....

2...
....

3...
....

Today I:

[] Did 15 minutes of exercise
[] Sat quietly and relaxed (meditation)
[] Was kind to someone.
How?...
[] Spent time in nature
[] Listened to my favourite song
[] Ate something healthy
[] Called a friend
[] Hugged someone
[] Completed an unfinished task. What was
   it?..
[] Started/worked on a hobby
[] Read a few pages of a great book
[] Took photos of something beautiful
[] Started to learn a new skill
[] Laughed at something really funny

Today was fun
because..
....
....

Happiness rating:

1 2 3 4 5 6 7 8 9 10

Day 170

I am grateful for:

1...
....

2...
....

3...
....

Today I:

[] Did 15 minutes of exercise
[] Sat quietly and relaxed (meditation)
[] Was kind to someone.
How?...
[] Spent time in nature
[] Listened to my favourite song
[] Ate something healthy
[] Called a friend
[] Hugged someone
[] Completed an unfinished task. What was
   it?...
[] Started/worked on a hobby
[] Read a few pages of a great book
[] Took photos of something beautiful
[] Started to learn a new skill
[] Laughed at something really funny

Today was fun
because...
....
....

Happiness rating:

 1 2 3 4 5 6 7 8 9 10

Day 171

I am grateful for:
1...
....

2...
....

3...
....

Today I:

[] Did 15 minutes of exercise
[] Sat quietly and relaxed (meditation)
[] Was kind to someone.
How?...
[] Spent time in nature
[] Listened to my favourite song
[] Ate something healthy
[] Called a friend
[] Hugged someone
[] Completed an unfinished task. What was
   it?..
[] Started/worked on a hobby
[] Read a few pages of a great book
[] Took photos of something beautiful
[] Started to learn a new skill
[] Laughed at something really funny

Today was fun
because...
....
....

Happiness rating:

        1 2 3 4 5 6 7 8 9 10

Day 172

I am grateful for:

1......................................
....

2......................................
....

3......................................
....

Today I:

[] Did 15 minutes of exercise
[] Sat quietly and relaxed (meditation)
[] Was kind to someone.
How?..................................
[] Spent time in nature
[] Listened to my favourite song
[] Ate something healthy
[] Called a friend
[] Hugged someone
[] Completed an unfinished task. What was
   it?..............................
[] Started/worked on a hobby
[] Read a few pages of a great book
[] Took photos of something beautiful
[] Started to learn a new skill
[] Laughed at something really funny

Today was fun
because..............................
....
....

Happiness rating:

1 2 3 4 5 6 7 8 9 10

Day 173

I am grateful for:

1..
....

2..
....

3..
....

Today I:

[] Did 15 minutes of exercise
[] Sat quietly and relaxed (meditation)
[] Was kind to someone.
How?..
[] Spent time in nature
[] Listened to my favourite song
[] Ate something healthy
[] Called a friend
[] Hugged someone
[] Completed an unfinished task. What was
    it?..
[] Started/worked on a hobby
[] Read a few pages of a great book
[] Took photos of something beautiful
[] Started to learn a new skill
[] Laughed at something really funny

Today was fun
because.......................................
....
....

Happiness rating:

        1 2 3 4 5 6 7 8 9 10

Day 174

I am grateful for:

1...
....

2...
....

3...
....

Today I:

[] Did 15 minutes of exercise
[] Sat quietly and relaxed (meditation)
[] Was kind to someone.
How?.......................................
[] Spent time in nature
[] Listened to my favourite song
[] Ate something healthy
[] Called a friend
[] Hugged someone
[] Completed an unfinished task. What was
    it?..
[] Started/worked on a hobby
[] Read a few pages of a great book
[] Took photos of something beautiful
[] Started to learn a new skill
[] Laughed at something really funny

Today was fun
because...................................
....
....

Happiness rating:

1 2 3 4 5 6 7 8 9 10

Day 175

I am grateful for:

1...
....

2...
....

3...
....

Today I:

[] Did 15 minutes of exercise
[] Sat quietly and relaxed (meditation)
[] Was kind to someone.
How?...
[] Spent time in nature
[] Listened to my favourite song
[] Ate something healthy
[] Called a friend
[] Hugged someone
[] Completed an unfinished task. What was
   it?.......................................
[] Started/worked on a hobby
[] Read a few pages of a great book
[] Took photos of something beautiful
[] Started to learn a new skill
[] Laughed at something really funny

Today was fun
because.......................................
....
....

Happiness rating:

         1 2 3 4 5 6 7 8 9 10

Staying happy on social media

Social media can be a very happy place to visit. Chatting with your friends, checking out each other's photos and playing games are fun things to do. Unfortunately, it can become a negative space too, so with the aim of focusing on happiness, here are some tips on how to stay happy on social media:

1. Positive posting. Share posts that are fun, funny, happy and light. This will help you, and your friends will enjoy it too.
2. If you don't have anything nice to say, don't say anything. Avoid gossip, complaining and criticising, and try not to get involved in negative conversations.
3. Keep your fights offline. If you are arguing with someone, it's best to do it in person, as it's very easy to mistake someone's tone in a typed message.
4. Have family members and close friends (people that really care for you) as your social media friends.
5. Take a break. Don't spend all your time online; enjoy the moment you're in with the people you're with, in person!
6. Don't take it personally. Other people's lives can look extremely interesting on social media, but that's because they only post the most interesting bits. Everyone's lives look more interesting online.

Hint
Don't forget: you control it (not the other way around), so if things go really wrong, just don't log in! You can even cancel your account.

Day 176

I am grateful for:
1...
....
2...
....
3...
....

Today I:

[] Did 15 minutes of exercise
[] Sat quietly and relaxed (meditation)
[] Was kind to someone.
How?.......................................
[] Spent time in nature
[] Listened to my favourite song
[] Ate something healthy
[] Called a friend
[] Hugged someone
[] Completed an unfinished task. What was
   it?......................................
[] Started/worked on a hobby
[] Read a few pages of a great book
[] Took photos of something beautiful
[] Started to learn a new skill
[] Laughed at something really funny

Today was fun
because....................................
....
....

Happiness rating:

1 2 3 4 5 6 7 8 9 10

Day 177

I am grateful for:

1...
....
2...
....
3...
....

Today I:

[] Did 15 minutes of exercise
[] Sat quietly and relaxed (meditation)
[] Was kind to someone.
How?.......................................
[] Spent time in nature
[] Listened to my favourite song
[] Ate something healthy
[] Called a friend
[] Hugged someone
[] Completed an unfinished task. What was
   it?.....................................
[] Started/worked on a hobby
[] Read a few pages of a great book
[] Took photos of something beautiful
[] Started to learn a new skill
[] Laughed at something really funny

Today was fun
because.....................................
....
....

Happiness rating:

        1 2 3 4 5 6 7 8 9 10

Day 178

I am grateful for:

1...
....

2...
....

3...
....

Today I:

[] Did 15 minutes of exercise
[] Sat quietly and relaxed (meditation)
[] Was kind to someone.
How?......................................
[] Spent time in nature
[] Listened to my favourite song
[] Ate something healthy
[] Called a friend
[] Hugged someone
[] Completed an unfinished task. What was
   it?....................................
[] Started/worked on a hobby
[] Read a few pages of a great book
[] Took photos of something beautiful
[] Started to learn a new skill
[] Laughed at something really funny

Today was fun
because...................................
....
....

Happiness rating:

     1 2 3 4 5 6 7 8 9 10

Day 179

I am grateful for:
1...
....
2...
....
3...
....

Today I:

[] Did 15 minutes of exercise
[] Sat quietly and relaxed (meditation)
[] Was kind to someone.
How?..
[] Spent time in nature
[] Listened to my favourite song
[] Ate something healthy
[] Called a friend
[] Hugged someone
[] Completed an unfinished task. What was
   it?..
[] Started/worked on a hobby
[] Read a few pages of a great book
[] Took photos of something beautiful
[] Started to learn a new skill
[] Laughed at something really funny

Today was fun
because...
....
....

Happiness rating:

    1 2 3 4 5 6 7 8 9 10

Day 180

I am grateful for:

1..
....

2..
....

3..
....

Today I:

[] Did 15 minutes of exercise
[] Sat quietly and relaxed (meditation)
[] Was kind to someone.
How?......................................
[] Spent time in nature
[] Listened to my favourite song
[] Ate something healthy
[] Called a friend
[] Hugged someone
[] Completed an unfinished task. What was
   it?....................................
[] Started/worked on a hobby
[] Read a few pages of a great book
[] Took photos of something beautiful
[] Started to learn a new skill
[] Laughed at something really funny

Today was fun
because...................................
....
....

Happiness rating:

1 2 3 4 5 6 7 8 9 10

Day 181

I am grateful for:

1..
....

2..
....

3..
....

Today I:

[] Did 15 minutes of exercise
[] Sat quietly and relaxed (meditation)
[] Was kind to someone.
How?...
[] Spent time in nature
[] Listened to my favourite song
[] Ate something healthy
[] Called a friend
[] Hugged someone
[] Completed an unfinished task. What was
   it?..
[] Started/worked on a hobby
[] Read a few pages of a great book
[] Took photos of something beautiful
[] Started to learn a new skill
[] Laughed at something really funny

Today was fun
because.......................................
....
....

Happiness rating:

     1 2 3 4 5 6 7 8 9 10

Day 182

I am grateful for:

1..
....

2..
....

3..
....

Today I:

[] Did 15 minutes of exercise
[] Sat quietly and relaxed (meditation)
[] Was kind to someone.
How?......................................
[] Spent time in nature
[] Listened to my favourite song
[] Ate something healthy
[] Called a friend
[] Hugged someone
[] Completed an unfinished task. What was
   it?....................................
[] Started/worked on a hobby
[] Read a few pages of a great book
[] Took photos of something beautiful
[] Started to learn a new skill
[] Laughed at something really funny

Today was fun
because...................................
....
....

Happiness rating:

        1 2 3 4 5 6 7 8 9 10

"Celebrate the happiness that friends are always giving, make every day a holiday and celebrate just living!"

Amanda Bradley

Day 183

I am grateful for:

1..
....

2..
....

3..
....

Today I:

[] Did 15 minutes of exercise
[] Sat quietly and relaxed (meditation)
[] Was kind to someone.
How?......................................
[] Spent time in nature
[] Listened to my favourite song
[] Ate something healthy
[] Called a friend
[] Hugged someone
[] Completed an unfinished task. What was
    it?....................................
[] Started/worked on a hobby
[] Read a few pages of a great book
[] Took photos of something beautiful
[] Started to learn a new skill
[] Laughed at something really funny

Today was fun
because...................................
....
....

Happiness rating:

   1 2 3 4 5 6 7 8 9 10

Day 184

I am grateful for:

1..
....

2..
....

3..
....

Today I:

[] Did 15 minutes of exercise
[] Sat quietly and relaxed (meditation)
[] Was kind to someone.
How?..
[] Spent time in nature
[] Listened to my favourite song
[] Ate something healthy
[] Called a friend
[] Hugged someone
[] Completed an unfinished task. What was
   it?......................................
[] Started/worked on a hobby
[] Read a few pages of a great book
[] Took photos of something beautiful
[] Started to learn a new skill
[] Laughed at something really funny

Today was fun
because.....................................
....
....

Happiness rating:

        1 2 3 4 5 6 7 8 9 10

Day 185

I am grateful for:

1...
....

2...
....

3...
....

Today I:

[] Did 15 minutes of exercise
[] Sat quietly and relaxed (meditation)
[] Was kind to someone.
How?..
[] Spent time in nature
[] Listened to my favourite song
[] Ate something healthy
[] Called a friend
[] Hugged someone
[] Completed an unfinished task. What was
   it?......................................
[] Started/worked on a hobby
[] Read a few pages of a great book
[] Took photos of something beautiful
[] Started to learn a new skill
[] Laughed at something really funny

Today was fun
because.....................................
....
....

Happiness rating:

         1 2 3 4 5 6 7 8 9 10

Day 186

I am grateful for:

1...
....

2...
....

3...
....

Today I:

[] Did 15 minutes of exercise
[] Sat quietly and relaxed (meditation)
[] Was kind to someone.
How?.......................................
[] Spent time in nature
[] Listened to my favourite song
[] Ate something healthy
[] Called a friend
[] Hugged someone
[] Completed an unfinished task. What was
   it?......................................
[] Started/worked on a hobby
[] Read a few pages of a great book
[] Took photos of something beautiful
[] Started to learn a new skill
[] Laughed at something really funny

Today was fun
because....................................
....
....

Happiness rating:

    1 2 3 4 5 6 7 8 9 10

Day 187

I am grateful for:

1...
....

2...
....

3...
....

Today I:

[] Did 15 minutes of exercise
[] Sat quietly and relaxed (meditation)
[] Was kind to someone.
How?..
[] Spent time in nature
[] Listened to my favourite song
[] Ate something healthy
[] Called a friend
[] Hugged someone
[] Completed an unfinished task. What was
   it?......................................
[] Started/worked on a hobby
[] Read a few pages of a great book
[] Took photos of something beautiful
[] Started to learn a new skill
[] Laughed at something really funny

Today was fun
because.....................................
....
....

Happiness rating:

        1 2 3 4 5 6 7 8 9 10

Day 188

I am grateful for:

1..
....

2..
....

3..
....

Today I:

[] Did 15 minutes of exercise
[] Sat quietly and relaxed (meditation)
[] Was kind to someone.
How?...
[] Spent time in nature
[] Listened to my favourite song
[] Ate something healthy
[] Called a friend
[] Hugged someone
[] Completed an unfinished task. What was
   it?...
[] Started/worked on a hobby
[] Read a few pages of a great book
[] Took photos of something beautiful
[] Started to learn a new skill
[] Laughed at something really funny

Today was fun
because..
....
....

Happiness rating:

         1   2   3   4   5   6   7   8   9   10

Day 189

I am grateful for:
1..
....

2..
....

3..
....

Today I:

[] Did 15 minutes of exercise
[] Sat quietly and relaxed (meditation)
[] Was kind to someone.
How?..
[] Spent time in nature
[] Listened to my favourite song
[] Ate something healthy
[] Called a friend
[] Hugged someone
[] Completed an unfinished task. What was
   it?.....................................
[] Started/worked on a hobby
[] Read a few pages of a great book
[] Took photos of something beautiful
[] Started to learn a new skill
[] Laughed at something really funny

Today was fun
because......................................
....
....

Happiness rating:

         1 2 3 4 5 6 7 8 9 10

Great Expectations

When I started researching expectations and happiness I got really confused. Some people were saying I needed to have really low expectations so I could be happy WHATEVER happened, and others said to 'reach for the stars' and expect only the best. Expectations are important; let's face it, no one would achieve anything without having goals, making plans and placing some expectations on themselves. However, expecting something or someone to be a certain way can limit your experience, and your happiness.

Your expectations, or the way you believe your life should be, are closely related to how happy you can be. If your life 'matches' or exceeds the picture you have, then you are likely to be very happy. If it doesn't match, then you probably won't be. Here you get to make a choice.

1. You can feel unhappy and blame others. (Not ideal.)
2. You can figure out how to change your life to meet your expectations.
3. You can change your expectations.

Remember, it is your choice.

Hint
Break it down. There are probably some areas of your life that do match your expectations, and some that don't.

Tony Robbins (2013), *The Secret of Happiness*.
www.youtube.com

Day 190

I am grateful for:

1..
....

2..
....

3..
....

Today I:

[] Did 15 minutes of exercise
[] Sat quietly and relaxed (meditation)
[] Was kind to someone.
How?..
[] Spent time in nature
[] Listened to my favourite song
[] Ate something healthy
[] Called a friend
[] Hugged someone
[] Completed an unfinished task. What was
    it?..
[] Started/worked on a hobby
[] Read a few pages of a great book
[] Took photos of something beautiful
[] Started to learn a new skill
[] Laughed at something really funny

Today was fun
because.......................................
....
....

Happiness rating:

        1 2 3 4 5 6 7 8 9 10

Day 191

I am grateful for:

1..
....

2..
....

3..
....

Today I:

[] Did 15 minutes of exercise
[] Sat quietly and relaxed (meditation)
[] Was kind to someone.
How?....................................
[] Spent time in nature
[] Listened to my favourite song
[] Ate something healthy
[] Called a friend
[] Hugged someone
[] Completed an unfinished task. What was
   it?....................................
[] Started/worked on a hobby
[] Read a few pages of a great book
[] Took photos of something beautiful
[] Started to learn a new skill
[] Laughed at something really funny

Today was fun
because..................................
....
....

Happiness rating:

1   2   3   4   5   6   7   8   9   10

Day 192

I am grateful for:

1..
....

2..
....

3..
....

Today I:

[] Did 15 minutes of exercise
[] Sat quietly and relaxed (meditation)
[] Was kind to someone.
How?...
[] Spent time in nature
[] Listened to my favourite song
[] Ate something healthy
[] Called a friend
[] Hugged someone
[] Completed an unfinished task. What was
    it?.......................................
[] Started/worked on a hobby
[] Read a few pages of a great book
[] Took photos of something beautiful
[] Started to learn a new skill
[] Laughed at something really funny

Today was fun
because.......................................
....
....

Happiness rating:

        1 2 3 4 5 6 7 8 9 10

Day 193

I am grateful for:

1..
....

2..
....

3..
....

Today I:

[] Did 15 minutes of exercise
[] Sat quietly and relaxed (meditation)
[] Was kind to someone.
How?......................................
[] Spent time in nature
[] Listened to my favourite song
[] Ate something healthy
[] Called a friend
[] Hugged someone
[] Completed an unfinished task. What was
   it?....................................
[] Started/worked on a hobby
[] Read a few pages of a great book
[] Took photos of something beautiful
[] Started to learn a new skill
[] Laughed at something really funny

Today was fun
because...................................
....
....

Happiness rating:

        1 2 3 4 5 6 7 8 9 10

Day 194

I am grateful for:
1..
....
2..
....
3..
....

Today I:

[] Did 15 minutes of exercise
[] Sat quietly and relaxed (meditation)
[] Was kind to someone.
How?...
[] Spent time in nature
[] Listened to my favourite song
[] Ate something healthy
[] Called a friend
[] Hugged someone
[] Completed an unfinished task. What was
   it?..
[] Started/worked on a hobby
[] Read a few pages of a great book
[] Took photos of something beautiful
[] Started to learn a new skill
[] Laughed at something really funny

Today was fun
because......................................
....
....

Happiness rating:

    1 2 3 4 5 6 7 8 9 10

Day 195

I am grateful for:

1...
....

2...
....

3...
....

Today I:

[] Did 15 minutes of exercise
[] Sat quietly and relaxed (meditation)
[] Was kind to someone.
How?.......................................
[] Spent time in nature
[] Listened to my favourite song
[] Ate something healthy
[] Called a friend
[] Hugged someone
[] Completed an unfinished task. What was
    it?.....................................
[] Started/worked on a hobby
[] Read a few pages of a great book
[] Took photos of something beautiful
[] Started to learn a new skill
[] Laughed at something really funny

Today was fun
because....................................
....
....

Happiness rating:

        1 2 3 4 5 6 7 8 9 10

Day 196

I am grateful for:

1...
....

2...
....

3...
....

Today I:

[] Did 15 minutes of exercise
[] Sat quietly and relaxed (meditation)
[] Was kind to someone.
How?...
[] Spent time in nature
[] Listened to my favourite song
[] Ate something healthy
[] Called a friend
[] Hugged someone
[] Completed an unfinished task. What was
    it?...
[] Started/worked on a hobby
[] Read a few pages of a great book
[] Took photos of something beautiful
[] Started to learn a new skill
[] Laughed at something really funny

Today was fun
because..
....
....

Happiness rating:

        1 2 3 4 5 6 7 8 9 10

"No matter how many mistakes you make, or how slow you progress, you're still way ahead of everyone who isn't trying."

Tony Robbins

Keep going...

Day 197

I am grateful for:

1..
....

2..
....

3..
....

Today I:

[] Did 15 minutes of exercise
[] Sat quietly and relaxed (meditation)
[] Was kind to someone.
How?.......................................
[] Spent time in nature
[] Listened to my favourite song
[] Ate something healthy
[] Called a friend
[] Hugged someone
[] Completed an unfinished task. What was
   it?......................................
[] Started/worked on a hobby
[] Read a few pages of a great book
[] Took photos of something beautiful
[] Started to learn a new skill
[] Laughed at something really funny

Today was fun
because....................................
....
....

Happiness rating:

1 2 3 4 5 6 7 8 9 10

Day 198

I am grateful for:

1...
....

2...
....

3...
....

Today I:

[] Did 15 minutes of exercise
[] Sat quietly and relaxed (meditation)
[] Was kind to someone.
How?......................................
[] Spent time in nature
[] Listened to my favourite song
[] Ate something healthy
[] Called a friend
[] Hugged someone
[] Completed an unfinished task. What was
   it?....................................
[] Started/worked on a hobby
[] Read a few pages of a great book
[] Took photos of something beautiful
[] Started to learn a new skill
[] Laughed at something really funny

Today was fun
because....................................
....
....

Happiness rating:

1   2   3   4   5   6   7   8   9   10

Day 199

I am grateful for:

1..
....

2..
....

3..
....

Today I:

[] Did 15 minutes of exercise
[] Sat quietly and relaxed (meditation)
[] Was kind to someone.
How?...
[] Spent time in nature
[] Listened to my favourite song
[] Ate something healthy
[] Called a friend
[] Hugged someone
[] Completed an unfinished task. What was
   it?...
[] Started/worked on a hobby
[] Read a few pages of a great book
[] Took photos of something beautiful
[] Started to learn a new skill
[] Laughed at something really funny

Today was fun
because..
....
....

Happiness rating:

         1 2 3 4 5 6 7 8 9 10

Day 200

I am grateful for:
1...
....

2...
....

3...
....

Today I:

[] Did 15 minutes of exercise
[] Sat quietly and relaxed (meditation)
[] Was kind to someone.
How?.....................................
[] Spent time in nature
[] Listened to my favourite song
[] Ate something healthy
[] Called a friend
[] Hugged someone
[] Completed an unfinished task. What was
   it?...................................
[] Started/worked on a hobby
[] Read a few pages of a great book
[] Took photos of something beautiful
[] Started to learn a new skill
[] Laughed at something really funny

Today was fun
because..................................
....
....

Happiness rating:

        1 2 3 4 5 6 7 8 9 10

Day 201

I am grateful for:

1..

....

2..

....

3..

....

Today I:

[] Did 15 minutes of exercise
[] Sat quietly and relaxed (meditation)
[] Was kind to someone.
How?..
[] Spent time in nature
[] Listened to my favourite song
[] Ate something healthy
[] Called a friend
[] Hugged someone
[] Completed an unfinished task. What was
    it?..
[] Started/worked on a hobby
[] Read a few pages of a great book
[] Took photos of something beautiful
[] Started to learn a new skill
[] Laughed at something really funny

Today was fun
because...
....
....

Happiness rating:

1   2   3   4   5   6   7   8   9   10

Day 202

I am grateful for:

1...
....

2...
....

3...
....

Today I:

[] Did 15 minutes of exercise
[] Sat quietly and relaxed (meditation)
[] Was kind to someone.
How?...
[] Spent time in nature
[] Listened to my favourite song
[] Ate something healthy
[] Called a friend
[] Hugged someone
[] Completed an unfinished task. What was
   it?..
[] Started/worked on a hobby
[] Read a few pages of a great book
[] Took photos of something beautiful
[] Started to learn a new skill
[] Laughed at something really funny

Today was fun
because..
....
....

Happiness rating:

        1 2 3 4 5 6 7 8 9 10

Day 203

I am grateful for:
1..
....

2..
....

3..
....

Today I:

[] Did 15 minutes of exercise
[] Sat quietly and relaxed (meditation)
[] Was kind to someone.
How?......................................
[] Spent time in nature
[] Listened to my favourite song
[] Ate something healthy
[] Called a friend
[] Hugged someone
[] Completed an unfinished task. What was
    it?....................................
[] Started/worked on a hobby
[] Read a few pages of a great book
[] Took photos of something beautiful
[] Started to learn a new skill
[] Laughed at something really funny

Today was fun
because...................................
....
....

Happiness rating:

        1 2 3 4 5 6 7 8 9 10

Unfinished Business

Messy room, chores left undone, homework
list as long as your arm, music practice,
sports training, unreturned library books,
an unfulfilled promise…
Make you feel slightly queasy?
That's because these things are all
incomplete tasks, or unfinished business.
Leaving things undone can really hold you
back, keep you thinking about the past, and
even cause guilty feelings.
It naturally goes that completing your tasks
will stop you feeling guilty, help you focus
on other (more important) things, and enjoy
the present.
Jeff Olson (2013 Kindle Edition), The *Slight Edge*.
Greenleaf Book Press

If tackling that pile seems like an
impossible task then here's a few ideas to
help:

1. Write it all down. Making a list stops
you having to constantly think about your
tasks, and helps you decide which order to
do them in. (Or whether to do them at all!)
2. Make a plan. The act of making a plan to
deal with an unfinished task will help your
brain move on.
3. Every little helps! Don't feel that you
have to complete everything in one day (that
can be overwhelming).
4. Get started. Pick something and do it!
5. Make it a habit. Use this journal as a
reminder, and tick the box once you're done.

Day 204

I am grateful for:

1...
....

2...
....

3...
....

Today I:

[] Did 15 minutes of exercise
[] Sat quietly and relaxed (meditation)
[] Was kind to someone.
How?.......................................
[] Spent time in nature
[] Listened to my favourite song
[] Ate something healthy
[] Called a friend
[] Hugged someone
[] Completed an unfinished task. What was
   it?.....................................
[] Started/worked on a hobby
[] Read a few pages of a great book
[] Took photos of something beautiful
[] Started to learn a new skill
[] Laughed at something really funny

Today was fun
because....................................
....
....

Happiness rating:

1 2 3 4 5 6 7 8 9 10

Day 205

I am grateful for:

1..
....

2..
....

3..
....

Today I:

[] Did 15 minutes of exercise
[] Sat quietly and relaxed (meditation)
[] Was kind to someone.
How?...
[] Spent time in nature
[] Listened to my favourite song
[] Ate something healthy
[] Called a friend
[] Hugged someone
[] Completed an unfinished task. What was
   it?..
[] Started/worked on a hobby
[] Read a few pages of a great book
[] Took photos of something beautiful
[] Started to learn a new skill
[] Laughed at something really funny

Today was fun
because......................................
....
....

Happiness rating:

1 2 3 4 5 6 7 8 9 10

Day 206

I am grateful for:

1..
....

2..
....

3..
....

Today I:

[] Did 15 minutes of exercise
[] Sat quietly and relaxed (meditation)
[] Was kind to someone.
How?...
[] Spent time in nature
[] Listened to my favourite song
[] Ate something healthy
[] Called a friend
[] Hugged someone
[] Completed an unfinished task. What was
   it?.......................................
[] Started/worked on a hobby
[] Read a few pages of a great book
[] Took photos of something beautiful
[] Started to learn a new skill
[] Laughed at something really funny

Today was fun
because.......................................
....
....

Happiness rating:

   1 2 3 4 5 6 7 8 9 10

Day 207

I am grateful for:

1..
....

2..
....

3..
....

Today I:

[] Did 15 minutes of exercise
[] Sat quietly and relaxed (meditation)
[] Was kind to someone.
How?.......................................
[] Spent time in nature
[] Listened to my favourite song
[] Ate something healthy
[] Called a friend
[] Hugged someone
[] Completed an unfinished task. What was
   it?.....................................
[] Started/worked on a hobby
[] Read a few pages of a great book
[] Took photos of something beautiful
[] Started to learn a new skill
[] Laughed at something really funny

Today was fun
because....................................
....
....

Happiness rating:

    1 2 3 4 5 6 7 8 9 10

Day 208

I am grateful for:

1...
....

2...
....

3...
....

Today I:

[] Did 15 minutes of exercise
[] Sat quietly and relaxed (meditation)
[] Was kind to someone.
How?...
[] Spent time in nature
[] Listened to my favourite song
[] Ate something healthy
[] Called a friend
[] Hugged someone
[] Completed an unfinished task. What was
   it?...
[] Started/worked on a hobby
[] Read a few pages of a great book
[] Took photos of something beautiful
[] Started to learn a new skill
[] Laughed at something really funny

Today was fun
because..
....
....

Happiness rating:

      1 2 3 4 5 6 7 8 9 10

Day 209

I am grateful for:

1..
....

2..
....

3..
....

Today I:

[] Did 15 minutes of exercise
[] Sat quietly and relaxed (meditation)
[] Was kind to someone.
How?...
[] Spent time in nature
[] Listened to my favourite song
[] Ate something healthy
[] Called a friend
[] Hugged someone
[] Completed an unfinished task. What was
   it?..
[] Started/worked on a hobby
[] Read a few pages of a great book
[] Took photos of something beautiful
[] Started to learn a new skill
[] Laughed at something really funny

Today was fun
because......................................
....
....

Happiness rating:

        1 2 3 4 5 6 7 8 9 10

Day 210

I am grateful for:
1..
....
2..
....
3..
....

Today I:

[] Did 15 minutes of exercise
[] Sat quietly and relaxed (meditation)
[] Was kind to someone.
How?...
[] Spent time in nature
[] Listened to my favourite song
[] Ate something healthy
[] Called a friend
[] Hugged someone
[] Completed an unfinished task. What was
    it?..
[] Started/worked on a hobby
[] Read a few pages of a great book
[] Took photos of something beautiful
[] Started to learn a new skill
[] Laughed at something really funny

Today was fun
because..
....
....

Happiness rating:

        1 2 3 4 5 6 7 8 9 10

You are brave!

Day 211

I am grateful for:

1..
....

2..
....

3..
....

Today I:

[] Did 15 minutes of exercise
[] Sat quietly and relaxed (meditation)
[] Was kind to someone.
How?......................................
[] Spent time in nature
[] Listened to my favourite song
[] Ate something healthy
[] Called a friend
[] Hugged someone
[] Completed an unfinished task. What was
   it?......................................
[] Started/worked on a hobby
[] Read a few pages of a great book
[] Took photos of something beautiful
[] Started to learn a new skill
[] Laughed at something really funny

Today was fun
because......................................
....
....

Happiness rating:

    1 2 3 4 5 6 7 8 9 10

Day 212

I am grateful for:

1...
....

2...
....

3...
....

Today I:

[] Did 15 minutes of exercise
[] Sat quietly and relaxed (meditation)
[] Was kind to someone.
How?......................................
[] Spent time in nature
[] Listened to my favourite song
[] Ate something healthy
[] Called a friend
[] Hugged someone
[] Completed an unfinished task. What was
   it?....................................
[] Started/worked on a hobby
[] Read a few pages of a great book
[] Took photos of something beautiful
[] Started to learn a new skill
[] Laughed at something really funny

Today was fun
because....................................
....
....

Happiness rating:

1 2 3 4 5 6 7 8 9 10

Day 213

I am grateful for:

1..
....

2..
....

3..
....

Today I:

[] Did 15 minutes of exercise
[] Sat quietly and relaxed (meditation)
[] Was kind to someone.
How?...
[] Spent time in nature
[] Listened to my favourite song
[] Ate something healthy
[] Called a friend
[] Hugged someone
[] Completed an unfinished task. What was
   it?..
[] Started/worked on a hobby
[] Read a few pages of a great book
[] Took photos of something beautiful
[] Started to learn a new skill
[] Laughed at something really funny

Today was fun
because.......................................
....
....

Happiness rating:

    1 2 3 4 5 6 7 8 9 10

Day 214

I am grateful for:

1..
....

2..
....

3..
....

Today I:

[] Did 15 minutes of exercise
[] Sat quietly and relaxed (meditation)
[] Was kind to someone.
How?...
[] Spent time in nature
[] Listened to my favourite song
[] Ate something healthy
[] Called a friend
[] Hugged someone
[] Completed an unfinished task. What was
   it?..
[] Started/worked on a hobby
[] Read a few pages of a great book
[] Took photos of something beautiful
[] Started to learn a new skill
[] Laughed at something really funny

Today was fun
because......................................
....
....

Happiness rating:

     1 2 3 4 5 6 7 8 9 10

Day 215

I am grateful for:

1..
....

2..
....

3..
....

Today I:

[] Did 15 minutes of exercise
[] Sat quietly and relaxed (meditation)
[] Was kind to someone.
How?......................................
[] Spent time in nature
[] Listened to my favourite song
[] Ate something healthy
[] Called a friend
[] Hugged someone
[] Completed an unfinished task. What was
   it?....................................
[] Started/worked on a hobby
[] Read a few pages of a great book
[] Took photos of something beautiful
[] Started to learn a new skill
[] Laughed at something really funny

Today was fun
because...................................
....
....

Happiness rating:

        1 2 3 4 5 6 7 8 9 10

Day 216

I am grateful for:
1..
....
2..
....
3..
....

Today I:

[] Did 15 minutes of exercise
[] Sat quietly and relaxed (meditation)
[] Was kind to someone.
How?..
[] Spent time in nature
[] Listened to my favourite song
[] Ate something healthy
[] Called a friend
[] Hugged someone
[] Completed an unfinished task. What was
   it?..
[] Started/worked on a hobby
[] Read a few pages of a great book
[] Took photos of something beautiful
[] Started to learn a new skill
[] Laughed at something really funny

Today was fun
because.....................................
....
....

Happiness rating:

     1 2 3 4 5 6 7 8 9 10

Day 217

I am grateful for:
1..
....
2..
....
3..
....

Today I:

[] Did 15 minutes of exercise
[] Sat quietly and relaxed (meditation)
[] Was kind to someone.
How?.......................................
[] Spent time in nature
[] Listened to my favourite song
[] Ate something healthy
[] Called a friend
[] Hugged someone
[] Completed an unfinished task. What was
    it?.....................................
[] Started/worked on a hobby
[] Read a few pages of a great book
[] Took photos of something beautiful
[] Started to learn a new skill
[] Laughed at something really funny

Today was fun
because....................................
....
....

Happiness rating:

     1 2 3 4 5 6 7 8 9 10

Happy Hobbies

By definition, a hobby is something we do purely for pleasure. So it makes sense that making time to fit in a hobby can lead to greater happiness. Hobbies can give you something to be excited about and provide you with a positive kind of challenge, generating the satisfaction that comes from learning and mastering a new skill. They can also provide a break from your ordinary routine.

A new hobby can help you explore new interests, and find friends who are interested in the same things. A hobby can even help you better enjoy time to yourself. Physically, hobbies reduce stress hormones, making you feel less tense and more relaxed.

Hint

The people who seem happiest in their long-term work are those that have taken a hobby they love, and turned it into their job or business.

Dani Dipirro (2013), 7 *Benefits of Having a Hobby.* www.positivelypresent.com

Day 218

I am grateful for:

1...
....

2...
....

3...
....

Today I:

[] Did 15 minutes of exercise
[] Sat quietly and relaxed (meditation)
[] Was kind to someone.
How?......................................
[] Spent time in nature
[] Listened to my favourite song
[] Ate something healthy
[] Called a friend
[] Hugged someone
[] Completed an unfinished task. What was
   it?....................................
[] Started/worked on a hobby
[] Read a few pages of a great book
[] Took photos of something beautiful
[] Started to learn a new skill
[] Laughed at something really funny

Today was fun
because....................................
....
....

Happiness rating:

    1 2 3 4 5 6 7 8 9 10

Day 219

I am grateful for:

1..
....

2..
....

3..
....

Today I:

[] Did 15 minutes of exercise
[] Sat quietly and relaxed (meditation)
[] Was kind to someone.
How?...
[] Spent time in nature
[] Listened to my favourite song
[] Ate something healthy
[] Called a friend
[] Hugged someone
[] Completed an unfinished task. What was
   it?..
[] Started/worked on a hobby
[] Read a few pages of a great book
[] Took photos of something beautiful
[] Started to learn a new skill
[] Laughed at something really funny

Today was fun
because......................................
....
....

Happiness rating:

1   2   3   4   5   6   7   8   9   10

Day 220

I am grateful for:

1...
....

2...
....

3...
....

Today I:

[] Did 15 minutes of exercise
[] Sat quietly and relaxed (meditation)
[] Was kind to someone.
How?...
[] Spent time in nature
[] Listened to my favourite song
[] Ate something healthy
[] Called a friend
[] Hugged someone
[] Completed an unfinished task. What was
   it?...
[] Started/worked on a hobby
[] Read a few pages of a great book
[] Took photos of something beautiful
[] Started to learn a new skill
[] Laughed at something really funny

Today was fun
because..
....
....

Happiness rating:

        1 2 3 4 5 6 7 8 9 10

Day 221

I am grateful for:
1..
....
2..
....
3..
....

Today I:

[] Did 15 minutes of exercise
[] Sat quietly and relaxed (meditation)
[] Was kind to someone.
How?...
[] Spent time in nature
[] Listened to my favourite song
[] Ate something healthy
[] Called a friend
[] Hugged someone
[] Completed an unfinished task. What was
    it?.......................................
[] Started/worked on a hobby
[] Read a few pages of a great book
[] Took photos of something beautiful
[] Started to learn a new skill
[] Laughed at something really funny

Today was fun
because......................................
....
....

Happiness rating:

        1 2 3 4 5 6 7 8 9 10

Day 222

I am grateful for:

1..
....

2..
....

3..
....

Today I:

[] Did 15 minutes of exercise
[] Sat quietly and relaxed (meditation)
[] Was kind to someone.
How?...
[] Spent time in nature
[] Listened to my favourite song
[] Ate something healthy
[] Called a friend
[] Hugged someone
[] Completed an unfinished task. What was
   it?...
[] Started/worked on a hobby
[] Read a few pages of a great book
[] Took photos of something beautiful
[] Started to learn a new skill
[] Laughed at something really funny

Today was fun
because..
....
....

Happiness rating:

    1 2 3 4 5 6 7 8 9 10

Day 223

I am grateful for:

1...
....

2...
....

3...
....

Today I:

[] Did 15 minutes of exercise
[] Sat quietly and relaxed (meditation)
[] Was kind to someone.
How?.......................................
[] Spent time in nature
[] Listened to my favourite song
[] Ate something healthy
[] Called a friend
[] Hugged someone
[] Completed an unfinished task. What was
   it?......................................
[] Started/worked on a hobby
[] Read a few pages of a great book
[] Took photos of something beautiful
[] Started to learn a new skill
[] Laughed at something really funny

Today was fun
because....................................
....
....

Happiness rating:

    1 2 3 4 5 6 7 8 9 10

266

Day 224

I am grateful for:

1..
....

2..
....

3..
....

Today I:

[] Did 15 minutes of exercise
[] Sat quietly and relaxed (meditation)
[] Was kind to someone.
How?...
[] Spent time in nature
[] Listened to my favourite song
[] Ate something healthy
[] Called a friend
[] Hugged someone
[] Completed an unfinished task. What was
   it?..
[] Started/worked on a hobby
[] Read a few pages of a great book
[] Took photos of something beautiful
[] Started to learn a new skill
[] Laughed at something really funny

Today was fun
because......................................
....
....

Happiness rating:

    1   2   3   4   5   6   7   8   9   10

Novel Ideas

A hobby can be anything you want. The key to hobby happiness is choosing something you really, really like (or think you'll like, it can be something new) and doing it just for fun! You never know where it could lead you!

1. Take up a new sport.

2. Learn to play a musical instrument.

3. Collect things. (Shells, rocks, toy cars... anything!)

4. Electronics. (Don't forget to ask someone before you pull something apart!)

5. Art of any kind.

6. Sew or knit or craft.

7. Take photos or make videos.

8. Dance!

9. Build models.

10. Write stories.

11. Learn to sing.

12. Read books.

13. Take up gardening.

14. Design and build your own... anything!

Day 225

I am grateful for:

1...
....

2...
....

3...
....

Today I:

[] Did 15 minutes of exercise
[] Sat quietly and relaxed (meditation)
[] Was kind to someone.
How?...
[] Spent time in nature
[] Listened to my favourite song
[] Ate something healthy
[] Called a friend
[] Hugged someone
[] Completed an unfinished task. What was
    it?.......................................
[] Started/worked on a hobby
[] Read a few pages of a great book
[] Took photos of something beautiful
[] Started to learn a new skill
[] Laughed at something really funny

Today was fun
because......................................
....
....

Happiness rating:

        1 2 3 4 5 6 7 8 9 10

Day 226

I am grateful for:

1..
....

2..
....

3..
....

Today I:

[] Did 15 minutes of exercise
[] Sat quietly and relaxed (meditation)
[] Was kind to someone.
How?...
[] Spent time in nature
[] Listened to my favourite song
[] Ate something healthy
[] Called a friend
[] Hugged someone
[] Completed an unfinished task. What was
   it?...
[] Started/worked on a hobby
[] Read a few pages of a great book
[] Took photos of something beautiful
[] Started to learn a new skill
[] Laughed at something really funny

Today was fun
because..
....
....

Happiness rating:

    1 2 3 4 5 6 7 8 9 10

Day 227

I am grateful for:

1..
....

2..
....

3..
....

Today I:

[] Did 15 minutes of exercise
[] Sat quietly and relaxed (meditation)
[] Was kind to someone.
How?...
[] Spent time in nature
[] Listened to my favourite song
[] Ate something healthy
[] Called a friend
[] Hugged someone
[] Completed an unfinished task. What was
   it?...
[] Started/worked on a hobby
[] Read a few pages of a great book
[] Took photos of something beautiful
[] Started to learn a new skill
[] Laughed at something really funny

Today was fun
because...
....
....

Happiness rating:

1 2 3 4 5 6 7 8 9 10

—— ——

Day 228

I am grateful for:

1...
....

2...
....

3...
....

Today I:

[] Did 15 minutes of exercise
[] Sat quietly and relaxed (meditation)
[] Was kind to someone.
How?..
[] Spent time in nature
[] Listened to my favourite song
[] Ate something healthy
[] Called a friend
[] Hugged someone
[] Completed an unfinished task. What was
   it?......................................
[] Started/worked on a hobby
[] Read a few pages of a great book
[] Took photos of something beautiful
[] Started to learn a new skill
[] Laughed at something really funny

Today was fun
because.....................................
....
....

Happiness rating:

    1 2 3 4 5 6 7 8 9 10

Day 229

I am grateful for:

1..
....

2..
....

3..
....

Today I:

[] Did 15 minutes of exercise
[] Sat quietly and relaxed (meditation)
[] Was kind to someone.
How?......................................
[] Spent time in nature
[] Listened to my favourite song
[] Ate something healthy
[] Called a friend
[] Hugged someone
[] Completed an unfinished task. What was
   it?....................................
[] Started/worked on a hobby
[] Read a few pages of a great book
[] Took photos of something beautiful
[] Started to learn a new skill
[] Laughed at something really funny

Today was fun
because...................................
....
....

Happiness rating:

1 2 3 4 5 6 7 8 9 10

Day 230

I am grateful for:

1......................................
....

2......................................
....

3......................................
....

Today I:

[] Did 15 minutes of exercise
[] Sat quietly and relaxed (meditation)
[] Was kind to someone.
How?..................................
[] Spent time in nature
[] Listened to my favourite song
[] Ate something healthy
[] Called a friend
[] Hugged someone
[] Completed an unfinished task. What was
   it?................................
[] Started/worked on a hobby
[] Read a few pages of a great book
[] Took photos of something beautiful
[] Started to learn a new skill
[] Laughed at something really funny

Today was fun
because................................
....
....

Happiness rating:

    1 2 3 4 5 6 7 8 9 10

Day 231

I am grateful for:

1..
....

2..
....

3..
....

Today I:

[] Did 15 minutes of exercise
[] Sat quietly and relaxed (meditation)
[] Was kind to someone.
How?..
[] Spent time in nature
[] Listened to my favourite song
[] Ate something healthy
[] Called a friend
[] Hugged someone
[] Completed an unfinished task. What was
   it?.......................................
[] Started/worked on a hobby
[] Read a few pages of a great book
[] Took photos of something beautiful
[] Started to learn a new skill
[] Laughed at something really funny

Today was fun
because.......................................
....
....

Happiness rating:

       1 2 3 4 5 6 7 8 9 10

"Find three hobbies you love: one to make you money, one to keep you in shape, and one to be creative."

Anonymous

Day 232

I am grateful for:

1..
....

2..
....

3..
....

Today I:

[] Did 15 minutes of exercise
[] Sat quietly and relaxed (meditation)
[] Was kind to someone.
How?...
[] Spent time in nature
[] Listened to my favourite song
[] Ate something healthy
[] Called a friend
[] Hugged someone
[] Completed an unfinished task. What was
    it?......................................
[] Started/worked on a hobby
[] Read a few pages of a great book
[] Took photos of something beautiful
[] Started to learn a new skill
[] Laughed at something really funny

Today was fun
because.......................................
....
....

Happiness rating:

         1 2 3 4 5 6 7 8 9 10

Day 233

I am grateful for:

1..
....
2..
....
3..
....

Today I:

[] Did 15 minutes of exercise
[] Sat quietly and relaxed (meditation)
[] Was kind to someone.
How?......................................
[] Spent time in nature
[] Listened to my favourite song
[] Ate something healthy
[] Called a friend
[] Hugged someone
[] Completed an unfinished task. What was
   it?....................................
[] Started/worked on a hobby
[] Read a few pages of a great book
[] Took photos of something beautiful
[] Started to learn a new skill
[] Laughed at something really funny

Today was fun
because...................................
....
....

Happiness rating:

        1 2 3 4 5 6 7 8 9 10

Day 234

I am grateful for:
1...
....

2...
....

3...
....

Today I:

[] Did 15 minutes of exercise
[] Sat quietly and relaxed (meditation)
[] Was kind to someone.
How?...
[] Spent time in nature
[] Listened to my favourite song
[] Ate something healthy
[] Called a friend
[] Hugged someone
[] Completed an unfinished task. What was
    it?...
[] Started/worked on a hobby
[] Read a few pages of a great book
[] Took photos of something beautiful
[] Started to learn a new skill
[] Laughed at something really funny

Today was fun
because...
....
....

Happiness rating:

    1 2 3 4 5 6 7 8 9 10

Day 235

I am grateful for:

1..
....

2..
....

3..
....

Today I:

[] Did 15 minutes of exercise
[] Sat quietly and relaxed (meditation)
[] Was kind to someone.
How?.......................................
[] Spent time in nature
[] Listened to my favourite song
[] Ate something healthy
[] Called a friend
[] Hugged someone
[] Completed an unfinished task. What was
   it?......................................
[] Started/worked on a hobby
[] Read a few pages of a great book
[] Took photos of something beautiful
[] Started to learn a new skill
[] Laughed at something really funny

Today was fun
because....................................
....
....

Happiness rating:

    1 2 3 4 5 6 7 8 9 10

Day 236

I am grateful for:

1...
....

2...
....

3...
....

Today I:

[] Did 15 minutes of exercise
[] Sat quietly and relaxed (meditation)
[] Was kind to someone.
How?..
[] Spent time in nature
[] Listened to my favourite song
[] Ate something healthy
[] Called a friend
[] Hugged someone
[] Completed an unfinished task. What was
   it?..
[] Started/worked on a hobby
[] Read a few pages of a great book
[] Took photos of something beautiful
[] Started to learn a new skill
[] Laughed at something really funny

Today was fun
because..
....
....

Happiness rating:

1   2   3   4   5   6   7   8   9   10

Day 237

I am grateful for:

1...
....

2...
....

3...
....

Today I:

[] Did 15 minutes of exercise
[] Sat quietly and relaxed (meditation)
[] Was kind to someone.
How?......................................
[] Spent time in nature
[] Listened to my favourite song
[] Ate something healthy
[] Called a friend
[] Hugged someone
[] Completed an unfinished task. What was
   it?......................................
[] Started/worked on a hobby
[] Read a few pages of a great book
[] Took photos of something beautiful
[] Started to learn a new skill
[] Laughed at something really funny

Today was fun
because....................................
....
....

Happiness rating:

        1 2 3 4 5 6 7 8 9 10

Day 238

I am grateful for:

1...
....

2...
....

3...
....

Today I:

[] Did 15 minutes of exercise
[] Sat quietly and relaxed (meditation)
[] Was kind to someone.
How?...
[] Spent time in nature
[] Listened to my favourite song
[] Ate something healthy
[] Called a friend
[] Hugged someone
[] Completed an unfinished task. What was
   it?..
[] Started/worked on a hobby
[] Read a few pages of a great book
[] Took photos of something beautiful
[] Started to learn a new skill
[] Laughed at something really funny

Today was fun
because..
....
....

Happiness rating:

     1 2 3 4 5 6 7 8 9 10

"Just keep swimming..."

Dory, *Finding Nemo*

(The Art of Perseverance)

Perseverance is the quality that allows you to keep doing something even though you may find it challenging.
Setbacks or 'failures' are actually a normal, acceptable part of life! The difference between the people that really succeed in life (whatever their version of success is) and those who don't is perseverance. They are not afraid keep trying because they're not afraid to fail.

And if they do fail...
They Just Keep Swimming (going)
Some of the world's most successful people have only 'made it' after monumental 'failures', or years of challenge.
Take J.K. Rowling: her first Harry Potter manuscript was rejected by 12 publishers before finally being accepted. Walt Disney's first cartoon production company went bankrupt, Oprah was sacked from her first TV reporting job for being 'unsuitable for television', and Michael Jordan was cut from his high school basketball team for 'lack of skill'. The list goes on. Henry Ford, Albert Einstein, Isaac Newton, Marilyn Monroe, Steve Jobs, Stephen Spielberg, Thomas Edison, and Stephen King all experienced massive challenges before finding their success.
They all had to keep persevering.
If any one of them had stopped trying, our world would look pretty different today.

"Failure is simply the opportunity to start again, this time more intelligently."

Henry Ford

"The key to success is failure."

Michael Jordan

Ruben Garcia (2013), *The Most Inspiring Famous Failures blog. megafounder.com*

Hint

Your goal for happiness could take time to reach. Sometimes you might trip up, have a sad day, or feel down. You might miss a day of happiness habits, or someone might just really annoy you. Don't worry. Don't give up even if it feels hard.

Just keep going.

Day 239

I am grateful for:

1......................................
....

2......................................
....

3......................................
....

Today I:

[] Did 15 minutes of exercise
[] Sat quietly and relaxed (meditation)
[] Was kind to someone.
How?...................................
[] Spent time in nature
[] Listened to my favourite song
[] Ate something healthy
[] Called a friend
[] Hugged someone
[] Completed an unfinished task. What was
   it?..................................
[] Started/worked on a hobby
[] Read a few pages of a great book
[] Took photos of something beautiful
[] Started to learn a new skill
[] Laughed at something really funny

Today was fun
because................................
....
....

Happiness rating:

1 2 3 4 5 6 7 8 9 10

Day 240

I am grateful for:
1..
....
2..
....
3..
....

Today I:

[] Did 15 minutes of exercise
[] Sat quietly and relaxed (meditation)
[] Was kind to someone.
How?......................................
[] Spent time in nature
[] Listened to my favourite song
[] Ate something healthy
[] Called a friend
[] Hugged someone
[] Completed an unfinished task. What was
   it?....................................
[] Started/worked on a hobby
[] Read a few pages of a great book
[] Took photos of something beautiful
[] Started to learn a new skill
[] Laughed at something really funny

Today was fun
because...................................
....
....

Happiness rating:

        1 2 3 4 5 6 7 8 9 10

Day 241

I am grateful for:

1...
....

2...
....

3...
....

Today I:

[] Did 15 minutes of exercise
[] Sat quietly and relaxed (meditation)
[] Was kind to someone.
How?......................................
[] Spent time in nature
[] Listened to my favourite song
[] Ate something healthy
[] Called a friend
[] Hugged someone
[] Completed an unfinished task. What was
   it?......................................
[] Started/worked on a hobby
[] Read a few pages of a great book
[] Took photos of something beautiful
[] Started to learn a new skill
[] Laughed at something really funny

Today was fun
because....................................
....
....

Happiness rating:

        1 2 3 4 5 6 7 8 9 10

Day 242

I am grateful for:

1..
....

2..
....

3..
....

Today I:

[] Did 15 minutes of exercise
[] Sat quietly and relaxed (meditation)
[] Was kind to someone.
How?..
[] Spent time in nature
[] Listened to my favourite song
[] Ate something healthy
[] Called a friend
[] Hugged someone
[] Completed an unfinished task. What was
    it?..
[] Started/worked on a hobby
[] Read a few pages of a great book
[] Took photos of something beautiful
[] Started to learn a new skill
[] Laughed at something really funny

Today was fun
because.......................................
....
....

Happiness rating:

         1 2 3 4 5 6 7 8 9 10

Day 243

I am grateful for:

1..
....

2..
....

3..
....

Today I:

[] Did 15 minutes of exercise
[] Sat quietly and relaxed (meditation)
[] Was kind to someone.
How?...
[] Spent time in nature
[] Listened to my favourite song
[] Ate something healthy
[] Called a friend
[] Hugged someone
[] Completed an unfinished task. What was
   it?...
[] Started/worked on a hobby
[] Read a few pages of a great book
[] Took photos of something beautiful
[] Started to learn a new skill
[] Laughed at something really funny

Today was fun
because..
....
....

Happiness rating:

1   2   3   4   5   6   7   8   9   10

Day 244

I am grateful for:

1..
....

2..
....

3..
....

Today I:

[] Did 15 minutes of exercise
[] Sat quietly and relaxed (meditation)
[] Was kind to someone.
How?..
[] Spent time in nature
[] Listened to my favourite song
[] Ate something healthy
[] Called a friend
[] Hugged someone
[] Completed an unfinished task. What was
    it?......................................
[] Started/worked on a hobby
[] Read a few pages of a great book
[] Took photos of something beautiful
[] Started to learn a new skill
[] Laughed at something really funny

Today was fun
because.....................................
....
....

Happiness rating:

        1 2 3 4 5 6 7 8 9 10

Day 245

I am grateful for:
1..
....
2..
....
3..
....

Today I:

[] Did 15 minutes of exercise
[] Sat quietly and relaxed (meditation)
[] Was kind to someone.
How?..
[] Spent time in nature
[] Listened to my favourite song
[] Ate something healthy
[] Called a friend
[] Hugged someone
[] Completed an unfinished task. What was
    it?...
[] Started/worked on a hobby
[] Read a few pages of a great book
[] Took photos of something beautiful
[] Started to learn a new skill
[] Laughed at something really funny

Today was fun
because...
....
....

Happiness rating:

        1 2 3 4 5 6 7 8 9 10

Grit Tips
(How to persevere)

1. Believe in yourself and your goal. Have a clear idea of what you want (here's where your happiness goal comes in handy) and know why you want to achieve it.

2. Use your imagination. See yourself already experiencing your happiness and success.

3. Famous failures. There are plenty of stories about people who have famously failed at something, only to turn themselves around and achieve personal success. Find a story you like to use as inspiration.

4. Celebrate small victories. Celebrating even the small 'wins' will help your brain notice your achievement and motivate you to keep going.

5. Try not to think negative thoughts. They will attempt to sneak in; notice them and let them go again.

6. Learn from your mistakes. Mistakes are normal, and can be a great opportunity to learn, and help you improve!

7. Don't listen to negative comments from people. Sometimes people try to pull you down without even knowing it, forgive them and move on.

8. Measure your progress. Occasionally look back to where you started, and realise how far you've come.

Day 246

I am grateful for:

1..
....
2..
....
3..
....

Today I:

[] Did 15 minutes of exercise
[] Sat quietly and relaxed (meditation)
[] Was kind to someone.
How?......................................
[] Spent time in nature
[] Listened to my favourite song
[] Ate something healthy
[] Called a friend
[] Hugged someone
[] Completed an unfinished task. What was
   it?.....................................
[] Started/worked on a hobby
[] Read a few pages of a great book
[] Took photos of something beautiful
[] Started to learn a new skill
[] Laughed at something really funny

Today was fun
because...................................
....
....

Happiness rating:

     1 2 3 4 5 6 7 8 9 10

Day 247

I am grateful for:

1..
....

2..
....

3..
....

Today I:

[] Did 15 minutes of exercise
[] Sat quietly and relaxed (meditation)
[] Was kind to someone.
How?..
[] Spent time in nature
[] Listened to my favourite song
[] Ate something healthy
[] Called a friend
[] Hugged someone
[] Completed an unfinished task. What was
    it?..
[] Started/worked on a hobby
[] Read a few pages of a great book
[] Took photos of something beautiful
[] Started to learn a new skill
[] Laughed at something really funny

Today was fun
because...
....
....

Happiness rating:

        1 2 3 4 5 6 7 8 9 10

Day 248

I am grateful for:

1..
....
2..
....
3..
....

Today I:

[] Did 15 minutes of exercise
[] Sat quietly and relaxed (meditation)
[] Was kind to someone.
How?...
[] Spent time in nature
[] Listened to my favourite song
[] Ate something healthy
[] Called a friend
[] Hugged someone
[] Completed an unfinished task. What was
   it?..
[] Started/worked on a hobby
[] Read a few pages of a great book
[] Took photos of something beautiful
[] Started to learn a new skill
[] Laughed at something really funny

Today was fun
because......................................
....
....

Happiness rating:

     1 2 3 4 5 6 7 8 9 10

Day 249

I am grateful for:

1...
....

2...
....

3...
....

Today I:

[] Did 15 minutes of exercise
[] Sat quietly and relaxed (meditation)
[] Was kind to someone.
How?...
[] Spent time in nature
[] Listened to my favourite song
[] Ate something healthy
[] Called a friend
[] Hugged someone
[] Completed an unfinished task. What was
    it?.......................................
[] Started/worked on a hobby
[] Read a few pages of a great book
[] Took photos of something beautiful
[] Started to learn a new skill
[] Laughed at something really funny

Today was fun
because.......................................
....
....

Happiness rating:

        1 2 3 4 5 6 7 8 9 10

Day 250

I am grateful for:

1...
....
2...
....
3...
....

Today I:

[] Did 15 minutes of exercise
[] Sat quietly and relaxed (meditation)
[] Was kind to someone.
How?......................................
[] Spent time in nature
[] Listened to my favourite song
[] Ate something healthy
[] Called a friend
[] Hugged someone
[] Completed an unfinished task. What was
   it?......................................
[] Started/worked on a hobby
[] Read a few pages of a great book
[] Took photos of something beautiful
[] Started to learn a new skill
[] Laughed at something really funny

Today was fun
because.....................................
....
....

Happiness rating:

1   2   3   4   5   6   7   8   9   10

Day 251

I am grateful for:

1...
....

2...
....

3...
....

Today I:

[] Did 15 minutes of exercise
[] Sat quietly and relaxed (meditation)
[] Was kind to someone.
How?..
[] Spent time in nature
[] Listened to my favourite song
[] Ate something healthy
[] Called a friend
[] Hugged someone
[] Completed an unfinished task. What was
    it?.....................................
[] Started/worked on a hobby
[] Read a few pages of a great book
[] Took photos of something beautiful
[] Started to learn a new skill
[] Laughed at something really funny

Today was fun
because.....................................
....
....

Happiness rating:

    1 2 3 4 5 6 7 8 9 10

Day 252

I am grateful for:
1..
....
2..
....
3..
....

Today I:

[] Did 15 minutes of exercise
[] Sat quietly and relaxed (meditation)
[] Was kind to someone.
How?......................................
[] Spent time in nature
[] Listened to my favourite song
[] Ate something healthy
[] Called a friend
[] Hugged someone
[] Completed an unfinished task. What was
   it?....................................
[] Started/worked on a hobby
[] Read a few pages of a great book
[] Took photos of something beautiful
[] Started to learn a new skill
[] Laughed at something really funny

Today was fun
because...................................
....
....

Happiness rating:

     1 2 3 4 5 6 7 8 9 10

"We don't need
magic to change
the world, we
carry all the
power we need
inside ourselves:
we have the power
to imagine
better."

J.K. Rowling

Day 253

I am grateful for:

1..
....

2..
....

3..
....

Today I:

[] Did 15 minutes of exercise
[] Sat quietly and relaxed (meditation)
[] Was kind to someone.
How?...
[] Spent time in nature
[] Listened to my favourite song
[] Ate something healthy
[] Called a friend
[] Hugged someone
[] Completed an unfinished task. What was
   it?..
[] Started/worked on a hobby
[] Read a few pages of a great book
[] Took photos of something beautiful
[] Started to learn a new skill
[] Laughed at something really funny

Today was fun
because...
....
....

Happiness rating:

1 2 3 4 5 6 7 8 9 10

Day 254

I am grateful for:
1..
....
2..
....
3..
....

Today I:

[] Did 15 minutes of exercise
[] Sat quietly and relaxed (meditation)
[] Was kind to someone.
How?..
[] Spent time in nature
[] Listened to my favourite song
[] Ate something healthy
[] Called a friend
[] Hugged someone
[] Completed an unfinished task. What was
    it?..
[] Started/worked on a hobby
[] Read a few pages of a great book
[] Took photos of something beautiful
[] Started to learn a new skill
[] Laughed at something really funny

Today was fun
because...
....
....

Happiness rating:

        1 2 3 4 5 6 7 8 9 10

Day 255

I am grateful for:

1..
....

2..
....

3..
....

Today I:

[] Did 15 minutes of exercise
[] Sat quietly and relaxed (meditation)
[] Was kind to someone.
How?......................................
[] Spent time in nature
[] Listened to my favourite song
[] Ate something healthy
[] Called a friend
[] Hugged someone
[] Completed an unfinished task. What was
    it?....................................
[] Started/worked on a hobby
[] Read a few pages of a great book
[] Took photos of something beautiful
[] Started to learn a new skill
[] Laughed at something really funny

Today was fun
because...................................
....
....

Happiness rating:

    1 2 3 4 5 6 7 8 9 10

Day 256

I am grateful for:
1..
....
2..
....
3..
....

Today I:

[] Did 15 minutes of exercise
[] Sat quietly and relaxed (meditation)
[] Was kind to someone.
How?..
[] Spent time in nature
[] Listened to my favourite song
[] Ate something healthy
[] Called a friend
[] Hugged someone
[] Completed an unfinished task. What was
    it?...
[] Started/worked on a hobby
[] Read a few pages of a great book
[] Took photos of something beautiful
[] Started to learn a new skill
[] Laughed at something really funny

Today was fun
because...
....
....

Happiness rating:

1   2   3   4   5   6   7   8   9   10

Day 257

I am grateful for:

1..
....

2..
....

3..
....

Today I:

[] Did 15 minutes of exercise
[] Sat quietly and relaxed (meditation)
[] Was kind to someone.
How?...
[] Spent time in nature
[] Listened to my favourite song
[] Ate something healthy
[] Called a friend
[] Hugged someone
[] Completed an unfinished task. What was
   it?.......................................
[] Started/worked on a hobby
[] Read a few pages of a great book
[] Took photos of something beautiful
[] Started to learn a new skill
[] Laughed at something really funny

Today was fun
because......................................
....
....

Happiness rating:

    1   2   3   4   5   6   7   8   9   10

Day 258

I am grateful for:

1..
....

2..
....

3..
....

Today I:

[] Did 15 minutes of exercise
[] Sat quietly and relaxed (meditation)
[] Was kind to someone.
How?...
[] Spent time in nature
[] Listened to my favourite song
[] Ate something healthy
[] Called a friend
[] Hugged someone
[] Completed an unfinished task. What was
    it?.......................................
[] Started/worked on a hobby
[] Read a few pages of a great book
[] Took photos of something beautiful
[] Started to learn a new skill
[] Laughed at something really funny

Today was fun
because.......................................
....
....

Happiness rating:

        1 2 3 4 5 6 7 8 9 10

Day 259

I am grateful for:

1......................................
....

2......................................
....

3......................................
....

Today I:

[] Did 15 minutes of exercise
[] Sat quietly and relaxed (meditation)
[] Was kind to someone.
How?....................................
[] Spent time in nature
[] Listened to my favourite song
[] Ate something healthy
[] Called a friend
[] Hugged someone
[] Completed an unfinished task. What was
   it?...................................
[] Started/worked on a hobby
[] Read a few pages of a great book
[] Took photos of something beautiful
[] Started to learn a new skill
[] Laughed at something really funny

Today was fun
because.................................
....
....

Happiness rating:

        1 2 3 4 5 6 7 8 9 10

Decisions, Decisions

You may not know it, but you make decisions that affect your life... every minute... every day. We all do!
And our decisions are powerful.
Even the little ones.
Especially when it comes to happiness.
What you decide to think about, or focus on, is what you decide to feel. Make sense? You also decide the meaning (whether it's good, bad, fun, boring). From there, you decide on your action, or what you're going to do...
The decisions you make, whether you know you're making them or not, dictate your experience. Made consciously, decisions can completely empower you. That is why practising gratitude and kindness are so important, as they are a decision to focus on the positive aspects of your life.
Negative stuff can happen too. In this case the choice to give it a more positive meaning, and to respond in a thoughtful way, can completely change your experience for the better. If you're mainly focusing on the negatives, you have the power to change your focus!
If you feel you've made the wrong decision about something, you can change that too!
It can take courage to notice and change your habits of thinking, but you can do it.
It really is your choice.
Tony Robbins (2013), *Decisions*
www.youtube.com

Hint
Everyone makes wrong decisions for themselves sometimes, and that's ok.
Just decide again!

Day 260

I am grateful for:

1..
....

2..
....

3..
....

Today I:

[] Did 15 minutes of exercise
[] Sat quietly and relaxed (meditation)
[] Was kind to someone.
How?.......................................
[] Spent time in nature
[] Listened to my favourite song
[] Ate something healthy
[] Called a friend
[] Hugged someone
[] Completed an unfinished task. What was
   it?.....................................
[] Started/worked on a hobby
[] Read a few pages of a great book
[] Took photos of something beautiful
[] Started to learn a new skill
[] Laughed at something really funny

Today was fun
because....................................
....
....

Happiness rating:

      1 2 3 4 5 6 7 8 9 10

Day 261

I am grateful for:

1..

....

2..

....

3..

....

Today I:

[] Did 15 minutes of exercise
[] Sat quietly and relaxed (meditation)
[] Was kind to someone.
How?...
[] Spent time in nature
[] Listened to my favourite song
[] Ate something healthy
[] Called a friend
[] Hugged someone
[] Completed an unfinished task. What was
    it?...
[] Started/worked on a hobby
[] Read a few pages of a great book
[] Took photos of something beautiful
[] Started to learn a new skill
[] Laughed at something really funny

Today was fun
because..

....

....

Happiness rating:

1 2 3 4 5 6 7 8 9 10

Day 262

I am grateful for:

1..
....

2..
....

3..
....

Today I:

[] Did 15 minutes of exercise
[] Sat quietly and relaxed (meditation)
[] Was kind to someone.
How?......................................
[] Spent time in nature
[] Listened to my favourite song
[] Ate something healthy
[] Called a friend
[] Hugged someone
[] Completed an unfinished task. What was
   it?......................................
[] Started/worked on a hobby
[] Read a few pages of a great book
[] Took photos of something beautiful
[] Started to learn a new skill
[] Laughed at something really funny

Today was fun
because...................................
....
....

Happiness rating:

        1 2 3 4 5 6 7 8 9 10

Day 263

I am grateful for:

1...
....

2...
....

3...
....

Today I:

[] Did 15 minutes of exercise
[] Sat quietly and relaxed (meditation)
[] Was kind to someone.
How?...
[] Spent time in nature
[] Listened to my favourite song
[] Ate something healthy
[] Called a friend
[] Hugged someone
[] Completed an unfinished task. What was
   it?.......................................
[] Started/worked on a hobby
[] Read a few pages of a great book
[] Took photos of something beautiful
[] Started to learn a new skill
[] Laughed at something really funny

Today was fun
because......................................
....
....

Happiness rating:

    1 2 3 4 5 6 7 8 9 10

313

Day 264

I am grateful for:

1..
....

2..
....

3..
....

Today I:

[] Did 15 minutes of exercise
[] Sat quietly and relaxed (meditation)
[] Was kind to someone.
How?..
[] Spent time in nature
[] Listened to my favourite song
[] Ate something healthy
[] Called a friend
[] Hugged someone
[] Completed an unfinished task. What was
   it?..
[] Started/worked on a hobby
[] Read a few pages of a great book
[] Took photos of something beautiful
[] Started to learn a new skill
[] Laughed at something really funny

Today was fun
because...
....
....

Happiness rating:

      1 2 3 4 5 6 7 8 9 10

Day 265

I am grateful for:

1..
....

2..
....

3..
....

Today I:

[] Did 15 minutes of exercise
[] Sat quietly and relaxed (meditation)
[] Was kind to someone.
How?....................................
[] Spent time in nature
[] Listened to my favourite song
[] Ate something healthy
[] Called a friend
[] Hugged someone
[] Completed an unfinished task. What was
    it?...................................
[] Started/worked on a hobby
[] Read a few pages of a great book
[] Took photos of something beautiful
[] Started to learn a new skill
[] Laughed at something really funny

Today was fun
because.................................
....
....

Happiness rating:

1 2 3 4 5 6 7 8 9 10

Day 266

I am grateful for:

1..
....

2..
....

3..
....

Today I:

[] Did 15 minutes of exercise
[] Sat quietly and relaxed (meditation)
[] Was kind to someone.
How?...
[] Spent time in nature
[] Listened to my favourite song
[] Ate something healthy
[] Called a friend
[] Hugged someone
[] Completed an unfinished task. What was
   it?..
[] Started/worked on a hobby
[] Read a few pages of a great book
[] Took photos of something beautiful
[] Started to learn a new skill
[] Laughed at something really funny

Today was fun
because..
....
....

Happiness rating:

          1 2 3 4 5 6 7 8 9 10

"Feel the fear and do it anyway!"

Susan Jeffers

Day 267

I am grateful for:

1..
....

2..
....

3..
....

Today I:

[] Did 15 minutes of exercise
[] Sat quietly and relaxed (meditation)
[] Was kind to someone.
How?......................................
[] Spent time in nature
[] Listened to my favourite song
[] Ate something healthy
[] Called a friend
[] Hugged someone
[] Completed an unfinished task. What was
   it?....................................
[] Started/worked on a hobby
[] Read a few pages of a great book
[] Took photos of something beautiful
[] Started to learn a new skill
[] Laughed at something really funny

Today was fun
because...................................
....
....

Happiness rating:

1 2 3 4 5 6 7 8 9 10

Day 268

I am grateful for:

1..
....

2..
....

3..
....

Today I:

[] Did 15 minutes of exercise
[] Sat quietly and relaxed (meditation)
[] Was kind to someone.
How?..
[] Spent time in nature
[] Listened to my favourite song
[] Ate something healthy
[] Called a friend
[] Hugged someone
[] Completed an unfinished task. What was
   it?..
[] Started/worked on a hobby
[] Read a few pages of a great book
[] Took photos of something beautiful
[] Started to learn a new skill
[] Laughed at something really funny

Today was fun
because..
....
....

Happiness rating:

1 2 3 4 5 6 7 8 9 10

Day 269

I am grateful for:

1..
....

2..
....

3..
....

Today I:

[] Did 15 minutes of exercise
[] Sat quietly and relaxed (meditation)
[] Was kind to someone.
How?...
[] Spent time in nature
[] Listened to my favourite song
[] Ate something healthy
[] Called a friend
[] Hugged someone
[] Completed an unfinished task. What was
   it?.......................................
[] Started/worked on a hobby
[] Read a few pages of a great book
[] Took photos of something beautiful
[] Started to learn a new skill
[] Laughed at something really funny

Today was fun
because.......................................
....
....

Happiness rating:

    1 2 3 4 5 6 7 8 9 10

Day 270

I am grateful for:

1...
....

2...
....

3...
....

Today I:

[] Did 15 minutes of exercise
[] Sat quietly and relaxed (meditation)
[] Was kind to someone.
How?...
[] Spent time in nature
[] Listened to my favourite song
[] Ate something healthy
[] Called a friend
[] Hugged someone
[] Completed an unfinished task. What was
   it?...
[] Started/worked on a hobby
[] Read a few pages of a great book
[] Took photos of something beautiful
[] Started to learn a new skill
[] Laughed at something really funny

Today was fun
because..
....
....

Happiness rating:

1 2 3 4 5 6 7 8 9 10

Day 271

I am grateful for:
1..
....
2..
....
3..
....

Today I:

[] Did 15 minutes of exercise
[] Sat quietly and relaxed (meditation)
[] Was kind to someone.
How?..
[] Spent time in nature
[] Listened to my favourite song
[] Ate something healthy
[] Called a friend
[] Hugged someone
[] Completed an unfinished task. What was
   it?.....................................
[] Started/worked on a hobby
[] Read a few pages of a great book
[] Took photos of something beautiful
[] Started to learn a new skill
[] Laughed at something really funny

Today was fun
because.....................................
....
....

Happiness rating:

   1 2 3 4 5 6 7 8 9 10

Day 272

I am grateful for:

1...
....

2...
....

3...
....

Today I:

[] Did 15 minutes of exercise
[] Sat quietly and relaxed (meditation)
[] Was kind to someone.
How?..
[] Spent time in nature
[] Listened to my favourite song
[] Ate something healthy
[] Called a friend
[] Hugged someone
[] Completed an unfinished task. What was
    it?..
[] Started/worked on a hobby
[] Read a few pages of a great book
[] Took photos of something beautiful
[] Started to learn a new skill
[] Laughed at something really funny

Today was fun
because......................................
....
....

Happiness rating:

1   2   3   4   5   6   7   8   9   10

Day 273

I am grateful for:
1..
....
2..
....
3..
....

Today I:

[] Did 15 minutes of exercise
[] Sat quietly and relaxed (meditation)
[] Was kind to someone.
How?......................................
[] Spent time in nature
[] Listened to my favourite song
[] Ate something healthy
[] Called a friend
[] Hugged someone
[] Completed an unfinished task. What was
   it?....................................
[] Started/worked on a hobby
[] Read a few pages of a great book
[] Took photos of something beautiful
[] Started to learn a new skill
[] Laughed at something really funny

Today was fun
because...................................
....
....

Happiness rating:

    1 2 3 4 5 6 7 8 9 10

The beauty of photography

Photographs are a fantastic way to remember great times, the people you love, places you've been, and the fun things you've done. Looking back at your photos and remembering the happy times can help you feel happier now!

Sharing photos with friends and family can bring you closer together, keep you up to date with each other, and help you relive happy memories.

You can also use photos to inspire you. Cut out pictures of places you really want to go and experiences you'd love to have and stick them on a pin board. Pinning up your own favourite pictures can also help remind you to smile. It's also great to use positive pictures as wallpaper on your devices.

But there's more!
The very act of taking photos can divert your focus from yourself and your worries, whether it's a happy face, pet, beautiful scenery, or a houseplant on the other side of the lens. It also literally 'focuses' your mind on how beautiful your surroundings are, keeps you connected with your environment, promotes creativity and encourages gratitude. This becomes even more powerful if you take photos with the intention of feeling happy!

Kurtz and Lyubomirsky (2013)

Hint
Make a scrapbook (digital or not) of your favourite shots!

Day 274

I am grateful for:

1...
....

2...
....

3...
....

Today I:

[] Did 15 minutes of exercise
[] Sat quietly and relaxed (meditation)
[] Was kind to someone.
How?..
[] Spent time in nature
[] Listened to my favourite song
[] Ate something healthy
[] Called a friend
[] Hugged someone
[] Completed an unfinished task. What was
   it?...
[] Started/worked on a hobby
[] Read a few pages of a great book
[] Took photos of something beautiful
[] Started to learn a new skill
[] Laughed at something really funny

Today was fun
because...
....
....

Happiness rating:

        1 2 3 4 5 6 7 8 9 10

Day 275

I am grateful for:

1..
....

2..
....

3..
....

Today I:

[] Did 15 minutes of exercise
[] Sat quietly and relaxed (meditation)
[] Was kind to someone.
How?..
[] Spent time in nature
[] Listened to my favourite song
[] Ate something healthy
[] Called a friend
[] Hugged someone
[] Completed an unfinished task. What was
    it?.....................................
[] Started/worked on a hobby
[] Read a few pages of a great book
[] Took photos of something beautiful
[] Started to learn a new skill
[] Laughed at something really funny

Today was fun
because.....................................
....
....

Happiness rating:

1 2 3 4 5 6 7 8 9 10

Day 276

I am grateful for:
1..
....
2..
....
3..
....

Today I:

[] Did 15 minutes of exercise
[] Sat quietly and relaxed (meditation)
[] Was kind to someone.
How?......................................
[] Spent time in nature
[] Listened to my favourite song
[] Ate something healthy
[] Called a friend
[] Hugged someone
[] Completed an unfinished task. What was
   it?.....................................
[] Started/worked on a hobby
[] Read a few pages of a great book
[] Took photos of something beautiful
[] Started to learn a new skill
[] Laughed at something really funny

Today was fun
because....................................
....
....

Happiness rating:

      1 2 3 4 5 6 7 8 9 10

Day 277

I am grateful for:

1..
....

2..
....

3..
....

Today I:

[] Did 15 minutes of exercise
[] Sat quietly and relaxed (meditation)
[] Was kind to someone.
How?......................................
[] Spent time in nature
[] Listened to my favourite song
[] Ate something healthy
[] Called a friend
[] Hugged someone
[] Completed an unfinished task. What was
   it?......................................
[] Started/worked on a hobby
[] Read a few pages of a great book
[] Took photos of something beautiful
[] Started to learn a new skill
[] Laughed at something really funny

Today was fun
because......................................
....
....

Happiness rating:

1 2 3 4 5 6 7 8 9 10

Day 278

I am grateful for:

1..

....

2..

....

3..

....

Today I:

[] Did 15 minutes of exercise
[] Sat quietly and relaxed (meditation)
[] Was kind to someone.
How?......................................
[] Spent time in nature
[] Listened to my favourite song
[] Ate something healthy
[] Called a friend
[] Hugged someone
[] Completed an unfinished task. What was
    it?......................................
[] Started/worked on a hobby
[] Read a few pages of a great book
[] Took photos of something beautiful
[] Started to learn a new skill
[] Laughed at something really funny

Today was fun
because......................................

....

....

Happiness rating:

     1 2 3 4 5 6 7 8 9 10

Day 279

I am grateful for:

1..
....

2..
....

3..
....

Today I:

[] Did 15 minutes of exercise
[] Sat quietly and relaxed (meditation)
[] Was kind to someone.
How?..
[] Spent time in nature
[] Listened to my favourite song
[] Ate something healthy
[] Called a friend
[] Hugged someone
[] Completed an unfinished task. What was
    it?...
[] Started/worked on a hobby
[] Read a few pages of a great book
[] Took photos of something beautiful
[] Started to learn a new skill
[] Laughed at something really funny

Today was fun
because...
....
....

Happiness rating:

1 2 3 4 5 6 7 8 9 10

Day 280

I am grateful for:

1..
....

2..
....

3..
....

Today I:

[] Did 15 minutes of exercise
[] Sat quietly and relaxed (meditation)
[] Was kind to someone.
How?...
[] Spent time in nature
[] Listened to my favourite song
[] Ate something healthy
[] Called a friend
[] Hugged someone
[] Completed an unfinished task. What was
   it?.......................................
[] Started/worked on a hobby
[] Read a few pages of a great book
[] Took photos of something beautiful
[] Started to learn a new skill
[] Laughed at something really funny

Today was fun
because.......................................
....
....

Happiness rating:

        1 2 3 4 5 6 7 8 9 10

Photo Spot

Stick a happy snap here!

Day 281

I am grateful for:

1..
....

2..
....

3..
....

Today I:

[] Did 15 minutes of exercise
[] Sat quietly and relaxed (meditation)
[] Was kind to someone.
How?...
[] Spent time in nature
[] Listened to my favourite song
[] Ate something healthy
[] Called a friend
[] Hugged someone
[] Completed an unfinished task. What was
   it?.......................................
[] Started/worked on a hobby
[] Read a few pages of a great book
[] Took photos of something beautiful
[] Started to learn a new skill
[] Laughed at something really funny

Today was fun
because......................................
....
....

Happiness rating:

      1 2 3 4 5 6 7 8 9 10

Day 282

I am grateful for:

1..
....

2..
....

3..
....

Today I:

[] Did 15 minutes of exercise
[] Sat quietly and relaxed (meditation)
[] Was kind to someone.
How?...
[] Spent time in nature
[] Listened to my favourite song
[] Ate something healthy
[] Called a friend
[] Hugged someone
[] Completed an unfinished task. What was
   it?..
[] Started/worked on a hobby
[] Read a few pages of a great book
[] Took photos of something beautiful
[] Started to learn a new skill
[] Laughed at something really funny

Today was fun
because.......................................
....
....

Happiness rating:

1 2 3 4 5 6 7 8 9 10

Day 283

I am grateful for:

1..
....

2..
....

3..
....

Today I:

[] Did 15 minutes of exercise
[] Sat quietly and relaxed (meditation)
[] Was kind to someone.
How?......................................
[] Spent time in nature
[] Listened to my favourite song
[] Ate something healthy
[] Called a friend
[] Hugged someone
[] Completed an unfinished task. What was
   it?.....................................
[] Started/worked on a hobby
[] Read a few pages of a great book
[] Took photos of something beautiful
[] Started to learn a new skill
[] Laughed at something really funny

Today was fun
because...................................
....
....

Happiness rating:

1 2 3 4 5 6 7 8 9 10

Day 284

I am grateful for:

1...
....

2...
....

3...
....

Today I:

[] Did 15 minutes of exercise
[] Sat quietly and relaxed (meditation)
[] Was kind to someone.
How?.......................................
[] Spent time in nature
[] Listened to my favourite song
[] Ate something healthy
[] Called a friend
[] Hugged someone
[] Completed an unfinished task. What was
   it?......................................
[] Started/worked on a hobby
[] Read a few pages of a great book
[] Took photos of something beautiful
[] Started to learn a new skill
[] Laughed at something really funny

Today was fun
because....................................
....
....

Happiness rating:

       1 2 3 4 5 6 7 8 9 10

Day 285

I am grateful for:

1..
....

2..
....

3..
....

Today I:

[] Did 15 minutes of exercise
[] Sat quietly and relaxed (meditation)
[] Was kind to someone.
How?......................................
[] Spent time in nature
[] Listened to my favourite song
[] Ate something healthy
[] Called a friend
[] Hugged someone
[] Completed an unfinished task. What was
    it?......................................
[] Started/worked on a hobby
[] Read a few pages of a great book
[] Took photos of something beautiful
[] Started to learn a new skill
[] Laughed at something really funny

Today was fun
because......................................
....
....

Happiness rating:

        1 2 3 4 5 6 7 8 9 10

Day 286

I am grateful for:

1..
....

2..
....

3..
....

Today I:

[] Did 15 minutes of exercise
[] Sat quietly and relaxed (meditation)
[] Was kind to someone.
How?..
[] Spent time in nature
[] Listened to my favourite song
[] Ate something healthy
[] Called a friend
[] Hugged someone
[] Completed an unfinished task. What was
   it?..
[] Started/worked on a hobby
[] Read a few pages of a great book
[] Took photos of something beautiful
[] Started to learn a new skill
[] Laughed at something really funny

Today was fun
because......................................
....
....

Happiness rating:

1   2   3   4   5   6   7   8   9   10

Day 287

I am grateful for:
1..
....
2..
....
3..
....

Today I:

[] Did 15 minutes of exercise
[] Sat quietly and relaxed (meditation)
[] Was kind to someone.
How?......................................
[] Spent time in nature
[] Listened to my favourite song
[] Ate something healthy
[] Called a friend
[] Hugged someone
[] Completed an unfinished task. What was
    it?......................................
[] Started/worked on a hobby
[] Read a few pages of a great book
[] Took photos of something beautiful
[] Started to learn a new skill
[] Laughed at something really funny

Today was fun
because......................................
....
....

Happiness rating:

        1 2 3 4 5 6 7 8 9 10

"The Earth is art, the photographer is only a witness."

Yann Arthus-Bertrand, *Earth from Above*

Day 288

I am grateful for:
1...
....
2...
....
3...
....

Today I:

[] Did 15 minutes of exercise
[] Sat quietly and relaxed (meditation)
[] Was kind to someone.
How?......................................
[] Spent time in nature
[] Listened to my favourite song
[] Ate something healthy
[] Called a friend
[] Hugged someone
[] Completed an unfinished task. What was
   it?.....................................
[] Started/worked on a hobby
[] Read a few pages of a great book
[] Took photos of something beautiful
[] Started to learn a new skill
[] Laughed at something really funny

Today was fun
because....................................
....
....

Happiness rating:

        1 2 3 4 5 6 7 8 9 10

Day 289

I am grateful for:

1...
....

2...
....

3...
....

Today I:

[] Did 15 minutes of exercise
[] Sat quietly and relaxed (meditation)
[] Was kind to someone.
How?.......................................
[] Spent time in nature
[] Listened to my favourite song
[] Ate something healthy
[] Called a friend
[] Hugged someone
[] Completed an unfinished task. What was
    it?.....................................
[] Started/worked on a hobby
[] Read a few pages of a great book
[] Took photos of something beautiful
[] Started to learn a new skill
[] Laughed at something really funny

Today was fun
because....................................
....
....

Happiness rating:

    1 2 3 4 5 6 7 8 9 10

Day 290

I am grateful for:

1...
....

2...
....

3...
....

Today I:

[] Did 15 minutes of exercise
[] Sat quietly and relaxed (meditation)
[] Was kind to someone.
How?..
[] Spent time in nature
[] Listened to my favourite song
[] Ate something healthy
[] Called a friend
[] Hugged someone
[] Completed an unfinished task. What was
   it?..
[] Started/worked on a hobby
[] Read a few pages of a great book
[] Took photos of something beautiful
[] Started to learn a new skill
[] Laughed at something really funny

Today was fun
because......................................
....
....

Happiness rating:

    1 2 3 4 5 6 7 8 9 10

Day 291

I am grateful for:

1..
....

2..
....

3..
....

Today I:

[] Did 15 minutes of exercise
[] Sat quietly and relaxed (meditation)
[] Was kind to someone.
How?..
[] Spent time in nature
[] Listened to my favourite song
[] Ate something healthy
[] Called a friend
[] Hugged someone
[] Completed an unfinished task. What was
   it?..
[] Started/worked on a hobby
[] Read a few pages of a great book
[] Took photos of something beautiful
[] Started to learn a new skill
[] Laughed at something really funny

Today was fun
because.......................................
....
....

Happiness rating:

        1 2 3 4 5 6 7 8 9 10

Day 292

I am grateful for:

1..
....

2..
....

3..
....

Today I:

[] Did 15 minutes of exercise
[] Sat quietly and relaxed (meditation)
[] Was kind to someone.
How?......................................
[] Spent time in nature
[] Listened to my favourite song
[] Ate something healthy
[] Called a friend
[] Hugged someone
[] Completed an unfinished task. What was
   it?.....................................
[] Started/worked on a hobby
[] Read a few pages of a great book
[] Took photos of something beautiful
[] Started to learn a new skill
[] Laughed at something really funny

Today was fun
because....................................
....
....

Happiness rating:

        1 2 3 4 5 6 7 8 9 10

Day 293

I am grateful for:

1..
....

2..
....

3..
....

Today I:

[] Did 15 minutes of exercise
[] Sat quietly and relaxed (meditation)
[] Was kind to someone.
How?..
[] Spent time in nature
[] Listened to my favourite song
[] Ate something healthy
[] Called a friend
[] Hugged someone
[] Completed an unfinished task. What was
   it?..
[] Started/worked on a hobby
[] Read a few pages of a great book
[] Took photos of something beautiful
[] Started to learn a new skill
[] Laughed at something really funny

Today was fun
because.....................................
....
....

Happiness rating:

    1 2 3 4 5 6 7 8 9 10

Day 294

I am grateful for:

1...
....

2...
....

3...
....

Today I:

[] Did 15 minutes of exercise
[] Sat quietly and relaxed (meditation)
[] Was kind to someone.
How?......................................
[] Spent time in nature
[] Listened to my favourite song
[] Ate something healthy
[] Called a friend
[] Hugged someone
[] Completed an unfinished task. What was
   it?......................................
[] Started/worked on a hobby
[] Read a few pages of a great book
[] Took photos of something beautiful
[] Started to learn a new skill
[] Laughed at something really funny

Today was fun
because......................................
....
....

Happiness rating:

       1 2 3 4 5 6 7 8 9 10

Solitude and secret spaces

What comes to mind when you think about solitude? Do you think of loneliness and sadness? Or contentment and happiness? Solitude is actually the ability to be alone and be completely happy about it! In a world where we are almost always connected to other people via the internet and social media, true solitude rarely happens, and being alone in any way is almost frowned upon. The irony is, we can be completely surrounded by people, either in person or online, and still feel completely lonely!

So how do we learn to enjoy solitude? Well some of the happiness practices in this book, like meditation, learning a new hobby or skill, listening to music, exercising or spending time in nature, are all great ways to create happy solitude.

Finding a space where you can go... your local park, beach, a tree in your back garden, or even your own bedroom can give you valuable time alone.

(Don't forget to let someone know where you're going.)

So why is solitude so important to our happiness? Alone time can help us unravel our problems and sort through complex emotions. It can also encourage original ideas and creativity and provide time for rest and recovery. Being positively alone can help you develop resilience and confidence, explore who you are, and give you energy and excitement for whatever comes next!

Esther Buchholz (1998), *The call of Solitude*.
www.psychologytoday.com

Day 295

I am grateful for:

1......................................
....

2......................................
....

3......................................
....

Today I:

[] Did 15 minutes of exercise
[] Sat quietly and relaxed (meditation)
[] Was kind to someone.
How?....................................
[] Spent time in nature
[] Listened to my favourite song
[] Ate something healthy
[] Called a friend
[] Hugged someone
[] Completed an unfinished task. What was
   it?..................................
[] Started/worked on a hobby
[] Read a few pages of a great book
[] Took photos of something beautiful
[] Started to learn a new skill
[] Laughed at something really funny

Today was fun
because.................................
....
....

Happiness rating:

     1 2 3 4 5 6 7 8 9 10

Day 296

I am grateful for:

1..
....

2..
....

3..
....

Today I:

[] Did 15 minutes of exercise
[] Sat quietly and relaxed (meditation)
[] Was kind to someone.
How?.......................................
[] Spent time in nature
[] Listened to my favourite song
[] Ate something healthy
[] Called a friend
[] Hugged someone
[] Completed an unfinished task. What was
    it?.....................................
[] Started/worked on a hobby
[] Read a few pages of a great book
[] Took photos of something beautiful
[] Started to learn a new skill
[] Laughed at something really funny

Today was fun
because.....................................
....
....

Happiness rating:

        1 2 3 4 5 6 7 8 9 10

Day 297

I am grateful for:

1..
....

2..
....

3..
....

Today I:

[] Did 15 minutes of exercise
[] Sat quietly and relaxed (meditation)
[] Was kind to someone.
How?......................................
[] Spent time in nature
[] Listened to my favourite song
[] Ate something healthy
[] Called a friend
[] Hugged someone
[] Completed an unfinished task. What was
   it?......................................
[] Started/worked on a hobby
[] Read a few pages of a great book
[] Took photos of something beautiful
[] Started to learn a new skill
[] Laughed at something really funny

Today was fun
because......................................
....
....

Happiness rating:

     1 2 3 4 5 6 7 8 9 10

Day 298

I am grateful for:

1...
....

2...
....

3...
....

Today I:

[] Did 15 minutes of exercise
[] Sat quietly and relaxed (meditation)
[] Was kind to someone.
How?.......................................
[] Spent time in nature
[] Listened to my favourite song
[] Ate something healthy
[] Called a friend
[] Hugged someone
[] Completed an unfinished task. What was
   it?.....................................
[] Started/worked on a hobby
[] Read a few pages of a great book
[] Took photos of something beautiful
[] Started to learn a new skill
[] Laughed at something really funny

Today was fun
because....................................
....
....

Happiness rating:

1   2   3   4   5   6   7   8   9   10

Day 299

I am grateful for:

1...
....
2...
....
3...
....

Today I:

[] Did 15 minutes of exercise
[] Sat quietly and relaxed (meditation)
[] Was kind to someone.
How?....................................
[] Spent time in nature
[] Listened to my favourite song
[] Ate something healthy
[] Called a friend
[] Hugged someone
[] Completed an unfinished task. What was
   it?...................................
[] Started/worked on a hobby
[] Read a few pages of a great book
[] Took photos of something beautiful
[] Started to learn a new skill
[] Laughed at something really funny

Today was fun
because.................................
....
....

Happiness rating:

     1 2 3 4 5 6 7 8 9 10

Day 300

I am grateful for:

1...
....

2...
....

3...
....

Today I:

[] Did 15 minutes of exercise
[] Sat quietly and relaxed (meditation)
[] Was kind to someone.
How?..
[] Spent time in nature
[] Listened to my favourite song
[] Ate something healthy
[] Called a friend
[] Hugged someone
[] Completed an unfinished task. What was
    it?..
[] Started/worked on a hobby
[] Read a few pages of a great book
[] Took photos of something beautiful
[] Started to learn a new skill
[] Laughed at something really funny

Today was fun
because.......................................
....
....

Happiness rating:

        1 2 3 4 5 6 7 8 9 10

Day 301

I am grateful for:

1..
....

2..
....

3..
....

Today I:

[] Did 15 minutes of exercise
[] Sat quietly and relaxed (meditation)
[] Was kind to someone.
How?.....................................
[] Spent time in nature
[] Listened to my favourite song
[] Ate something healthy
[] Called a friend
[] Hugged someone
[] Completed an unfinished task. What was
   it?...................................
[] Started/worked on a hobby
[] Read a few pages of a great book
[] Took photos of something beautiful
[] Started to learn a new skill
[] Laughed at something really funny

Today was fun
because..................................
....
....

Happiness rating:

        1 2 3 4 5 6 7 8 9 10

You are a Star!

Day 302

I am grateful for:

1..
....

2..
....

3..
....

Today I:

[] Did 15 minutes of exercise
[] Sat quietly and relaxed (meditation)
[] Was kind to someone.
How?...
[] Spent time in nature
[] Listened to my favourite song
[] Ate something healthy
[] Called a friend
[] Hugged someone
[] Completed an unfinished task. What was
   it?.......................................
[] Started/worked on a hobby
[] Read a few pages of a great book
[] Took photos of something beautiful
[] Started to learn a new skill
[] Laughed at something really funny

Today was fun
because.......................................
....
....

Happiness rating:

1   2   3   4   5   6   7   8   9   10

Day 303

I am grateful for:

1..
....

2..
....

3..
....

Today I:

[] Did 15 minutes of exercise
[] Sat quietly and relaxed (meditation)
[] Was kind to someone.
How?...
[] Spent time in nature
[] Listened to my favourite song
[] Ate something healthy
[] Called a friend
[] Hugged someone
[] Completed an unfinished task. What was
   it?..
[] Started/worked on a hobby
[] Read a few pages of a great book
[] Took photos of something beautiful
[] Started to learn a new skill
[] Laughed at something really funny

Today was fun
because.......................................
....
....

Happiness rating:

       1 2 3 4 5 6 7 8 9 10

Day 304

I am grateful for:

1..
....

2..
....

3..
....

Today I:

[] Did 15 minutes of exercise
[] Sat quietly and relaxed (meditation)
[] Was kind to someone.
How?......................................
[] Spent time in nature
[] Listened to my favourite song
[] Ate something healthy
[] Called a friend
[] Hugged someone
[] Completed an unfinished task. What was
   it?....................................
[] Started/worked on a hobby
[] Read a few pages of a great book
[] Took photos of something beautiful
[] Started to learn a new skill
[] Laughed at something really funny

Today was fun
because...................................
....
....

Happiness rating:

     1 2 3 4 5 6 7 8 9 10

Day 305

I am grateful for:

1...
....

2...
....

3...
....

Today I:

[] Did 15 minutes of exercise
[] Sat quietly and relaxed (meditation)
[] Was kind to someone.
How?.......................................
[] Spent time in nature
[] Listened to my favourite song
[] Ate something healthy
[] Called a friend
[] Hugged someone
[] Completed an unfinished task. What was
   it?......................................
[] Started/worked on a hobby
[] Read a few pages of a great book
[] Took photos of something beautiful
[] Started to learn a new skill
[] Laughed at something really funny

Today was fun
because....................................
....
....

Happiness rating:

1 2 3 4 5 6 7 8 9 10

Day 306

I am grateful for:
1..
....
2..
....
3..
....

Today I:

[] Did 15 minutes of exercise
[] Sat quietly and relaxed (meditation)
[] Was kind to someone.
How?....................................
[] Spent time in nature
[] Listened to my favourite song
[] Ate something healthy
[] Called a friend
[] Hugged someone
[] Completed an unfinished task. What was
   it?....................................
[] Started/worked on a hobby
[] Read a few pages of a great book
[] Took photos of something beautiful
[] Started to learn a new skill
[] Laughed at something really funny

Today was fun
because....................................
....
....

Happiness rating:

    1 2 3 4 5 6 7 8 9 10

Day 307

I am grateful for:

1..
....

2..
....

3..
....

Today I:

[] Did 15 minutes of exercise
[] Sat quietly and relaxed (meditation)
[] Was kind to someone.
How?..
[] Spent time in nature
[] Listened to my favourite song
[] Ate something healthy
[] Called a friend
[] Hugged someone
[] Completed an unfinished task. What was
    it?......................................
[] Started/worked on a hobby
[] Read a few pages of a great book
[] Took photos of something beautiful
[] Started to learn a new skill
[] Laughed at something really funny

Today was fun
because......................................
....
....

Happiness rating:

        1 2 3 4 5 6 7 8 9 10

Day 308

I am grateful for:

1..
....

2..
....

3..
....

Today I:

[] Did 15 minutes of exercise
[] Sat quietly and relaxed (meditation)
[] Was kind to someone.
How?......................................
[] Spent time in nature
[] Listened to my favourite song
[] Ate something healthy
[] Called a friend
[] Hugged someone
[] Completed an unfinished task. What was
   it?....................................
[] Started/worked on a hobby
[] Read a few pages of a great book
[] Took photos of something beautiful
[] Started to learn a new skill
[] Laughed at something really funny

Today was fun
because...................................
....
....

Happiness rating:

        1 2 3 4 5 6 7 8 9 10

Puppy Love

If you have a family pet, you will already know that spending time with an animal can bring immense fun and happiness! A pet can actually help reduce your stress, while also encouraging joy and playfulness.

A loving family pet provides unconditional love and affection, and can fulfil a need we have to touch and connect. This helps us to feel loved and accepted. Our pets can even help us meet new friends!

Pets, and dogs in particular, can ease the symptoms of anxiety. They help take your mind off your own worries, encourage you to go outside and exercise, and build your self-confidence. Plus, the routine required in caring for a pet can add structure to your day, and give you something to look forward to.

Even watching your fish swim around their tank, or the local bird and wildlife can be fun and relaxing.

Hint
If you don't, or can't, have a pet at home then you can spend time with a friend or neighbour's pet, visit your local zoo, community farm, or the countryside.

Lawrence and Segal (2016), The *Health Benefits of Dogs (and Cats)*.
www.helpguide.org

Day 309

I am grateful for:

1..
....
2..
....
3..
....

Today I:

[] Did 15 minutes of exercise
[] Sat quietly and relaxed (meditation)
[] Was kind to someone.
How?..
[] Spent time in nature
[] Listened to my favourite song
[] Ate something healthy
[] Called a friend
[] Hugged someone
[] Completed an unfinished task. What was
   it?......................................
[] Started/worked on a hobby
[] Read a few pages of a great book
[] Took photos of something beautiful
[] Started to learn a new skill
[] Laughed at something really funny

Today was fun
because.....................................
....
....

Happiness rating:

       1 2 3 4 5 6 7 8 9 10

Day 310

I am grateful for:

1..
....

2..
....

3..
....

Today I:

[] Did 15 minutes of exercise
[] Sat quietly and relaxed (meditation)
[] Was kind to someone.
How?...
[] Spent time in nature
[] Listened to my favourite song
[] Ate something healthy
[] Called a friend
[] Hugged someone
[] Completed an unfinished task. What was
   it?...
[] Started/worked on a hobby
[] Read a few pages of a great book
[] Took photos of something beautiful
[] Started to learn a new skill
[] Laughed at something really funny

Today was fun
because..
....
....

Happiness rating:

   1 2 3 4 5 6 7 8 9 10

Day 311

I am grateful for:

1...
....

2...
....

3...
....

Today I:

[] Did 15 minutes of exercise
[] Sat quietly and relaxed (meditation)
[] Was kind to someone.
How?.....................................
[] Spent time in nature
[] Listened to my favourite song
[] Ate something healthy
[] Called a friend
[] Hugged someone
[] Completed an unfinished task. What was
   it?....................................
[] Started/worked on a hobby
[] Read a few pages of a great book
[] Took photos of something beautiful
[] Started to learn a new skill
[] Laughed at something really funny

Today was fun
because..................................
....
....

Happiness rating:

    1 2 3 4 5 6 7 8 9 10

Day 312

I am grateful for:

1..
....

2..
....

3..
....

Today I:

[] Did 15 minutes of exercise
[] Sat quietly and relaxed (meditation)
[] Was kind to someone.
How?......................................
[] Spent time in nature
[] Listened to my favourite song
[] Ate something healthy
[] Called a friend
[] Hugged someone
[] Completed an unfinished task. What was
    it?......................................
[] Started/worked on a hobby
[] Read a few pages of a great book
[] Took photos of something beautiful
[] Started to learn a new skill
[] Laughed at something really funny

Today was fun
because....................................
....
....

Happiness rating:

        1 2 3 4 5 6 7 8 9 10

Day 313

I am grateful for:

1..
....

2..
....

3..
....

Today I:

[] Did 15 minutes of exercise
[] Sat quietly and relaxed (meditation)
[] Was kind to someone.
How?...
[] Spent time in nature
[] Listened to my favourite song
[] Ate something healthy
[] Called a friend
[] Hugged someone
[] Completed an unfinished task. What was
   it?..
[] Started/worked on a hobby
[] Read a few pages of a great book
[] Took photos of something beautiful
[] Started to learn a new skill
[] Laughed at something really funny

Today was fun
because......................................
....
....

Happiness rating:

     1 2 3 4 5 6 7 8 9 10

Day 314

I am grateful for:

1......................................
....

2......................................
....

3......................................
....

Today I:

[] Did 15 minutes of exercise
[] Sat quietly and relaxed (meditation)
[] Was kind to someone.
How?....................................
[] Spent time in nature
[] Listened to my favourite song
[] Ate something healthy
[] Called a friend
[] Hugged someone
[] Completed an unfinished task. What was
    it?..................................
[] Started/worked on a hobby
[] Read a few pages of a great book
[] Took photos of something beautiful
[] Started to learn a new skill
[] Laughed at something really funny

Today was fun
because.................................
....
....

Happiness rating:

   1 2 3 4 5 6 7 8 9 10

Day 315

I am grateful for:

1..
....

2..
....

3..
....

Today I:

[] Did 15 minutes of exercise
[] Sat quietly and relaxed (meditation)
[] Was kind to someone.
How?...
[] Spent time in nature
[] Listened to my favourite song
[] Ate something healthy
[] Called a friend
[] Hugged someone
[] Completed an unfinished task. What was
   it?.......................................
[] Started/worked on a hobby
[] Read a few pages of a great book
[] Took photos of something beautiful
[] Started to learn a new skill
[] Laughed at something really funny

Today was fun
because......................................
....
....

Happiness rating:

       1 2 3 4 5 6 7 8 9 10

"A dog doesn't care if you're rich or poor, educated or illiterate, clever or dull. Give him your heart and he will give you his."

John Grogan, *Marley and Me: Life and Love With the World's Worst Dog*

Day 316

I am grateful for:

1..
....

2..
....

3..
....

Today I:

[] Did 15 minutes of exercise
[] Sat quietly and relaxed (meditation)
[] Was kind to someone.
How?..
[] Spent time in nature
[] Listened to my favourite song
[] Ate something healthy
[] Called a friend
[] Hugged someone
[] Completed an unfinished task. What was
   it?..
[] Started/worked on a hobby
[] Read a few pages of a great book
[] Took photos of something beautiful
[] Started to learn a new skill
[] Laughed at something really funny

Today was fun
because......................................
....
....

Happiness rating:

    1 2 3 4 5 6 7 8 9 10

Day 317

I am grateful for:

1..
....

2..
....

3..
....

Today I:

[] Did 15 minutes of exercise
[] Sat quietly and relaxed (meditation)
[] Was kind to someone.
How?..
[] Spent time in nature
[] Listened to my favourite song
[] Ate something healthy
[] Called a friend
[] Hugged someone
[] Completed an unfinished task. What was
    it?......................................
[] Started/worked on a hobby
[] Read a few pages of a great book
[] Took photos of something beautiful
[] Started to learn a new skill
[] Laughed at something really funny

Today was fun
because......................................
....
....

Happiness rating:

    1 2 3 4 5 6 7 8 9 10

Day 318

I am grateful for:

1...
....

2...
....

3...
....

Today I:

[] Did 15 minutes of exercise
[] Sat quietly and relaxed (meditation)
[] Was kind to someone.
How?.....................................
[] Spent time in nature
[] Listened to my favourite song
[] Ate something healthy
[] Called a friend
[] Hugged someone
[] Completed an unfinished task. What was
   it?....................................
[] Started/worked on a hobby
[] Read a few pages of a great book
[] Took photos of something beautiful
[] Started to learn a new skill
[] Laughed at something really funny

Today was fun
because..................................
....
....

Happiness rating:

   1 2 3 4 5 6 7 8 9 10

Day 319

I am grateful for:

1..
....

2..
....

3..
....

Today I:

[] Did 15 minutes of exercise
[] Sat quietly and relaxed (meditation)
[] Was kind to someone.
How?.....................................
[] Spent time in nature
[] Listened to my favourite song
[] Ate something healthy
[] Called a friend
[] Hugged someone
[] Completed an unfinished task. What was
   it?...................................
[] Started/worked on a hobby
[] Read a few pages of a great book
[] Took photos of something beautiful
[] Started to learn a new skill
[] Laughed at something really funny

Today was fun
because..................................
....
....

Happiness rating:

        1 2 3 4 5 6 7 8 9 10

Day 320

I am grateful for:

1..
....

2..
....

3..
....

Today I:

[] Did 15 minutes of exercise
[] Sat quietly and relaxed (meditation)
[] Was kind to someone.
How?...
[] Spent time in nature
[] Listened to my favourite song
[] Ate something healthy
[] Called a friend
[] Hugged someone
[] Completed an unfinished task. What was
   it?...
[] Started/worked on a hobby
[] Read a few pages of a great book
[] Took photos of something beautiful
[] Started to learn a new skill
[] Laughed at something really funny

Today was fun
because..
....
....

Happiness rating:

1   2   3   4   5   6   7   8   9   10

Day 321

I am grateful for:

1..
....

2..
....

3..
....

Today I:

[] Did 15 minutes of exercise
[] Sat quietly and relaxed (meditation)
[] Was kind to someone.
How?......................................
[] Spent time in nature
[] Listened to my favourite song
[] Ate something healthy
[] Called a friend
[] Hugged someone
[] Completed an unfinished task. What was
    it?......................................
[] Started/worked on a hobby
[] Read a few pages of a great book
[] Took photos of something beautiful
[] Started to learn a new skill
[] Laughed at something really funny

Today was fun
because......................................
....
....

Happiness rating:

    1 2 3 4 5 6 7 8 9 10

Day 322

I am grateful for:
1..
....
2..
....
3..
....

Today I:

[] Did 15 minutes of exercise
[] Sat quietly and relaxed (meditation)
[] Was kind to someone.
How?...
[] Spent time in nature
[] Listened to my favourite song
[] Ate something healthy
[] Called a friend
[] Hugged someone
[] Completed an unfinished task. What was
   it?..
[] Started/worked on a hobby
[] Read a few pages of a great book
[] Took photos of something beautiful
[] Started to learn a new skill
[] Laughed at something really funny

Today was fun
because......................................
....
....

Happiness rating:

        1 2 3 4 5 6 7 8 9 10

Laughter IS the best medicine

Laughter has an amazing effect on our physical, mental and emotional health. Not only can a good laugh relieve stress, it can provide joy, and bring us closer to those we share it with.

Laughter is yet another way that your body releases endorphins, naturally making you feel good. It can boost your immune system, relax the muscles in your body and even relieve pain.

Humour can also help you through difficult situations, giving you optimism, courage and hope. With the ability to dissolve distressing emotions, laughter can 'shift your perspective' and help you see things in a more positive way.

And perhaps most importantly, laughter brings you closer to your loved ones and makes you feel good!

Smith and Segal (2016), *Laughter is the Best Medicine.* www.helpguide.org

A good laugh!

1. Watch a funny movie or TV show.
2. Tell jokes.
3. Make up silly stories.
4. Watch funny videos on YouTube!
5. Be silly with your friends.
6. Play a fun and funny game.

Day 323

I am grateful for:

1..
....

2..
....

3..
....

Today I:

[] Did 15 minutes of exercise
[] Sat quietly and relaxed (meditation)
[] Was kind to someone.
How?..
[] Spent time in nature
[] Listened to my favourite song
[] Ate something healthy
[] Called a friend
[] Hugged someone
[] Completed an unfinished task. What was
   it?......................................
[] Started/worked on a hobby
[] Read a few pages of a great book
[] Took photos of something beautiful
[] Started to learn a new skill
[] Laughed at something really funny

Today was fun
because......................................
....
....

Happiness rating:

        1 2 3 4 5 6 7 8 9 10

Day 324

I am grateful for:

1..
....

2..
....

3..
....

Today I:

[] Did 15 minutes of exercise
[] Sat quietly and relaxed (meditation)
[] Was kind to someone.
How?...
[] Spent time in nature
[] Listened to my favourite song
[] Ate something healthy
[] Called a friend
[] Hugged someone
[] Completed an unfinished task. What was
   it?..
[] Started/worked on a hobby
[] Read a few pages of a great book
[] Took photos of something beautiful
[] Started to learn a new skill
[] Laughed at something really funny

Today was fun
because.......................................
....
....

Happiness rating:

    1 2 3 4 5 6 7 8 9 10

Day 325

I am grateful for:

1...
....

2...
....

3...
....

Today I:

[] Did 15 minutes of exercise
[] Sat quietly and relaxed (meditation)
[] Was kind to someone.
How?...
[] Spent time in nature
[] Listened to my favourite song
[] Ate something healthy
[] Called a friend
[] Hugged someone
[] Completed an unfinished task. What was
   it?..
[] Started/worked on a hobby
[] Read a few pages of a great book
[] Took photos of something beautiful
[] Started to learn a new skill
[] Laughed at something really funny

Today was fun
because...
....
....

Happiness rating:

         1 2 3 4 5 6 7 8 9 10

Day 326

I am grateful for:

1..
....

2..
....

3..
....

Today I:

[] Did 15 minutes of exercise
[] Sat quietly and relaxed (meditation)
[] Was kind to someone.
How?.......................................
[] Spent time in nature
[] Listened to my favourite song
[] Ate something healthy
[] Called a friend
[] Hugged someone
[] Completed an unfinished task. What was
    it?......................................
[] Started/worked on a hobby
[] Read a few pages of a great book
[] Took photos of something beautiful
[] Started to learn a new skill
[] Laughed at something really funny

Today was fun
because......................................
....
....

Happiness rating:

    1 2 3 4 5 6 7 8 9 10

Day 327

I am grateful for:

1...
....

2...
....

3...
....

Today I:

[] Did 15 minutes of exercise
[] Sat quietly and relaxed (meditation)
[] Was kind to someone.
How?.....................................
[] Spent time in nature
[] Listened to my favourite song
[] Ate something healthy
[] Called a friend
[] Hugged someone
[] Completed an unfinished task. What was
   it?....................................
[] Started/worked on a hobby
[] Read a few pages of a great book
[] Took photos of something beautiful
[] Started to learn a new skill
[] Laughed at something really funny

Today was fun
because..................................
....
....

Happiness rating:

    1 2 3 4 5 6 7 8 9 10

___

Day 328

I am grateful for:

1...
....

2...
....

3...
....

Today I:

[] Did 15 minutes of exercise
[] Sat quietly and relaxed (meditation)
[] Was kind to someone.
How?...
[] Spent time in nature
[] Listened to my favourite song
[] Ate something healthy
[] Called a friend
[] Hugged someone
[] Completed an unfinished task. What was
   it?.......................................
[] Started/worked on a hobby
[] Read a few pages of a great book
[] Took photos of something beautiful
[] Started to learn a new skill
[] Laughed at something really funny

Today was fun
because...
....
....

Happiness rating:

        1 2 3 4 5 6 7 8 9 10

Day 329

I am grateful for:

1...
....

2...
....

3...
....

Today I:

[] Did 15 minutes of exercise
[] Sat quietly and relaxed (meditation)
[] Was kind to someone.
How?.....................................
[] Spent time in nature
[] Listened to my favourite song
[] Ate something healthy
[] Called a friend
[] Hugged someone
[] Completed an unfinished task. What was
   it?...................................
[] Started/worked on a hobby
[] Read a few pages of a great book
[] Took photos of something beautiful
[] Started to learn a new skill
[] Laughed at something really funny

Today was fun
because..................................
....
....

Happiness rating:

    1 2 3 4 5 6 7 8 9 10

"Laugh until your belly hurts, and then a little bit more!"

Katrina Mayer

Day 330

I am grateful for:

1..
....

2..
....

3..
....

Today I:

[] Did 15 minutes of exercise
[] Sat quietly and relaxed (meditation)
[] Was kind to someone.
How?...
[] Spent time in nature
[] Listened to my favourite song
[] Ate something healthy
[] Called a friend
[] Hugged someone
[] Completed an unfinished task. What was
   it?...
[] Started/worked on a hobby
[] Read a few pages of a great book
[] Took photos of something beautiful
[] Started to learn a new skill
[] Laughed at something really funny

Today was fun
because..
....
....

Happiness rating:

    1 2 3 4 5 6 7 8 9 10

Day 331

I am grateful for:
1...
....
2...
....
3...
....

Today I:

[] Did 15 minutes of exercise
[] Sat quietly and relaxed (meditation)
[] Was kind to someone.
How?..
[] Spent time in nature
[] Listened to my favourite song
[] Ate something healthy
[] Called a friend
[] Hugged someone
[] Completed an unfinished task. What was
    it?......................................
[] Started/worked on a hobby
[] Read a few pages of a great book
[] Took photos of something beautiful
[] Started to learn a new skill
[] Laughed at something really funny

Today was fun
because......................................
....
....

Happiness rating:

        1 2 3 4 5 6 7 8 9 10

Day 332

I am grateful for:
1..
....
2..
....
3..
....

Today I:

[] Did 15 minutes of exercise
[] Sat quietly and relaxed (meditation)
[] Was kind to someone.
How?...
[] Spent time in nature
[] Listened to my favourite song
[] Ate something healthy
[] Called a friend
[] Hugged someone
[] Completed an unfinished task. What was
   it?..
[] Started/worked on a hobby
[] Read a few pages of a great book
[] Took photos of something beautiful
[] Started to learn a new skill
[] Laughed at something really funny

Today was fun
because......................................
....
....

Happiness rating:

        1 2 3 4 5 6 7 8 9 10

Day 333

I am grateful for:

1..
....

2..
....

3..
....

Today I:

[] Did 15 minutes of exercise
[] Sat quietly and relaxed (meditation)
[] Was kind to someone.
How?..
[] Spent time in nature
[] Listened to my favourite song
[] Ate something healthy
[] Called a friend
[] Hugged someone
[] Completed an unfinished task. What was
   it?......................................
[] Started/worked on a hobby
[] Read a few pages of a great book
[] Took photos of something beautiful
[] Started to learn a new skill
[] Laughed at something really funny

Today was fun
because......................................
....
....

Happiness rating:

    1 2 3 4 5 6 7 8 9 10

Day 334

I am grateful for:

1...
....

2...
....

3...
....

Today I:

[] Did 15 minutes of exercise
[] Sat quietly and relaxed (meditation)
[] Was kind to someone.
How?......................................
[] Spent time in nature
[] Listened to my favourite song
[] Ate something healthy
[] Called a friend
[] Hugged someone
[] Completed an unfinished task. What was
   it?......................................
[] Started/worked on a hobby
[] Read a few pages of a great book
[] Took photos of something beautiful
[] Started to learn a new skill
[] Laughed at something really funny

Today was fun
because.....................................
....
....

Happiness rating:

      1 2 3 4 5 6 7 8 9 10

Day 335

I am grateful for:

1...
....

2...
....

3...
....

Today I:

[] Did 15 minutes of exercise
[] Sat quietly and relaxed (meditation)
[] Was kind to someone.
How?...
[] Spent time in nature
[] Listened to my favourite song
[] Ate something healthy
[] Called a friend
[] Hugged someone
[] Completed an unfinished task. What was
    it?...
[] Started/worked on a hobby
[] Read a few pages of a great book
[] Took photos of something beautiful
[] Started to learn a new skill
[] Laughed at something really funny

Today was fun
because..
....
....

Happiness rating:

    1   2   3   4   5   6   7   8   9   10

395

Day 336

I am grateful for:

1..
....

2..
....

3..
....

Today I:

[] Did 15 minutes of exercise
[] Sat quietly and relaxed (meditation)
[] Was kind to someone.
How?......................................
[] Spent time in nature
[] Listened to my favourite song
[] Ate something healthy
[] Called a friend
[] Hugged someone
[] Completed an unfinished task. What was
    it?....................................
[] Started/worked on a hobby
[] Read a few pages of a great book
[] Took photos of something beautiful
[] Started to learn a new skill
[] Laughed at something really funny

Today was fun
because...................................
....
....

Happiness rating:

    1   2   3   4   5   6   7   8   9   10

Skills for life

Learning a skill is simply the process of getting good at something! A new skill can be something you learn and do just for fun (hobby), for education or work, or to help you in everyday life. Whatever the purpose, skills can raise your confidence and empower you.
Simple skills like personal grooming, self-care and looking after your things will serve you well on a day-to-day basis. More complex skills like cooking and managing your money can be fun, interesting and extremely valuable.

You can become skilled at anything you like! Bike maintenance, electronics, cooking, finance, gardening, sewing, rock climbing... anything!!

So what can learning a new skill do for your happiness?

Aside from practical abilities, new skills can be rewarding, provide a positive challenge, and give you a sense of accomplishment and self-worth. This can lead to increased self-confidence, resilience and self-belief. You could even end up figuring out what you want to be or do in your future!!

Hint
Happiness is the skill you're learning right now!

Day 337

I am grateful for:

1..
....

2..
....

3..
....

Today I:

[] Did 15 minutes of exercise
[] Sat quietly and relaxed (meditation)
[] Was kind to someone.
How?..
[] Spent time in nature
[] Listened to my favourite song
[] Ate something healthy
[] Called a friend
[] Hugged someone
[] Completed an unfinished task. What was
   it?.....................................
[] Started/worked on a hobby
[] Read a few pages of a great book
[] Took photos of something beautiful
[] Started to learn a new skill
[] Laughed at something really funny

Today was fun
because.....................................
....
....

Happiness rating:

        1 2 3 4 5 6 7 8 9 10

Day 338

I am grateful for:

1..
....

2..
....

3..
....

Today I:

[] Did 15 minutes of exercise
[] Sat quietly and relaxed (meditation)
[] Was kind to someone.
How?......................................
[] Spent time in nature
[] Listened to my favourite song
[] Ate something healthy
[] Called a friend
[] Hugged someone
[] Completed an unfinished task. What was
    it?....................................
[] Started/worked on a hobby
[] Read a few pages of a great book
[] Took photos of something beautiful
[] Started to learn a new skill
[] Laughed at something really funny

Today was fun
because....................................
....
....

Happiness rating:

        1 2 3 4 5 6 7 8 9 10

Day 339

I am grateful for:

1..
....

2..
....

3..
....

Today I:

[] Did 15 minutes of exercise
[] Sat quietly and relaxed (meditation)
[] Was kind to someone.
How?......................................
[] Spent time in nature
[] Listened to my favourite song
[] Ate something healthy
[] Called a friend
[] Hugged someone
[] Completed an unfinished task. What was
   it?......................................
[] Started/worked on a hobby
[] Read a few pages of a great book
[] Took photos of something beautiful
[] Started to learn a new skill
[] Laughed at something really funny

Today was fun
because...................................
....
....

Happiness rating:

    1 2 3 4 5 6 7 8 9 10

Day 340

I am grateful for:
1..
....
2..
....
3..
....

Today I:

[] Did 15 minutes of exercise
[] Sat quietly and relaxed (meditation)
[] Was kind to someone.
How?...
[] Spent time in nature
[] Listened to my favourite song
[] Ate something healthy
[] Called a friend
[] Hugged someone
[] Completed an unfinished task. What was
    it?.......................................
[] Started/worked on a hobby
[] Read a few pages of a great book
[] Took photos of something beautiful
[] Started to learn a new skill
[] Laughed at something really funny

Today was fun
because......................................
....
....

Happiness rating:

        1 2 3 4 5 6 7 8 9 10

Day 341

I am grateful for:

1......................................
....

2......................................
....

3......................................
....

Today I:

[] Did 15 minutes of exercise
[] Sat quietly and relaxed (meditation)
[] Was kind to someone.
How?....................................
[] Spent time in nature
[] Listened to my favourite song
[] Ate something healthy
[] Called a friend
[] Hugged someone
[] Completed an unfinished task. What was
   it?....................................
[] Started/worked on a hobby
[] Read a few pages of a great book
[] Took photos of something beautiful
[] Started to learn a new skill
[] Laughed at something really funny

Today was fun
because.................................
....
....

Happiness rating:

1 2 3 4 5 6 7 8 9 10

Day 342

I am grateful for:
1...
....
2...
....
3...
....

Today I:

[] Did 15 minutes of exercise
[] Sat quietly and relaxed (meditation)
[] Was kind to someone.
How?..
[] Spent time in nature
[] Listened to my favourite song
[] Ate something healthy
[] Called a friend
[] Hugged someone
[] Completed an unfinished task. What was
   it?......................................
[] Started/worked on a hobby
[] Read a few pages of a great book
[] Took photos of something beautiful
[] Started to learn a new skill
[] Laughed at something really funny

Today was fun
because.....................................
....
....

Happiness rating:

        1 2 3 4 5 6 7 8 9 10

Day 343

I am grateful for:

1..
....

2..
....

3..
....

Today I:

[] Did 15 minutes of exercise
[] Sat quietly and relaxed (meditation)
[] Was kind to someone.
How?..
[] Spent time in nature
[] Listened to my favourite song
[] Ate something healthy
[] Called a friend
[] Hugged someone
[] Completed an unfinished task. What was
   it?......................................
[] Started/worked on a hobby
[] Read a few pages of a great book
[] Took photos of something beautiful
[] Started to learn a new skill
[] Laughed at something really funny

Today was fun
because......................................
....
....

Happiness rating:

        1 2 3 4 5 6 7 8 9 10

"All you need is 20 seconds of insane courage and I promise you something great will come of it."

We Bought a Zoo

Day 344

I am grateful for:

1..
....

2..
....

3..
....

Today I:

[] Did 15 minutes of exercise
[] Sat quietly and relaxed (meditation)
[] Was kind to someone.
How?..
[] Spent time in nature
[] Listened to my favourite song
[] Ate something healthy
[] Called a friend
[] Hugged someone
[] Completed an unfinished task. What was
   it?.......................................
[] Started/worked on a hobby
[] Read a few pages of a great book
[] Took photos of something beautiful
[] Started to learn a new skill
[] Laughed at something really funny

Today was fun
because.....................................
....
....

Happiness rating:

      1 2 3 4 5 6 7 8 9 10

Day 345

I am grateful for:

1..
....

2..
....

3..
....

Today I:

[] Did 15 minutes of exercise
[] Sat quietly and relaxed (meditation)
[] Was kind to someone.
How?..
[] Spent time in nature
[] Listened to my favourite song
[] Ate something healthy
[] Called a friend
[] Hugged someone
[] Completed an unfinished task. What was
   it?.....................................
[] Started/worked on a hobby
[] Read a few pages of a great book
[] Took photos of something beautiful
[] Started to learn a new skill
[] Laughed at something really funny

Today was fun
because.....................................
....
....

Happiness rating:

     1 2 3 4 5 6 7 8 9 10

Day 346

I am grateful for:

1...
....

2...
....

3...
....

Today I:

[] Did 15 minutes of exercise
[] Sat quietly and relaxed (meditation)
[] Was kind to someone.
How?.......................................
[] Spent time in nature
[] Listened to my favourite song
[] Ate something healthy
[] Called a friend
[] Hugged someone
[] Completed an unfinished task. What was
    it?.......................................
[] Started/worked on a hobby
[] Read a few pages of a great book
[] Took photos of something beautiful
[] Started to learn a new skill
[] Laughed at something really funny

Today was fun
because.......................................
....
....

Happiness rating:

        1 2 3 4 5 6 7 8 9 10

Day 347

I am grateful for:

1...
....

2...
....

3...
....

Today I:

[] Did 15 minutes of exercise
[] Sat quietly and relaxed (meditation)
[] Was kind to someone.
How?.....................................
[] Spent time in nature
[] Listened to my favourite song
[] Ate something healthy
[] Called a friend
[] Hugged someone
[] Completed an unfinished task. What was
   it?...................................
[] Started/worked on a hobby
[] Read a few pages of a great book
[] Took photos of something beautiful
[] Started to learn a new skill
[] Laughed at something really funny

Today was fun
because...................................
....
....

Happiness rating:

1 2 3 4 5 6 7 8 9 10

Day 348

I am grateful for:

1..
....

2..
....

3..
....

Today I:

[] Did 15 minutes of exercise
[] Sat quietly and relaxed (meditation)
[] Was kind to someone.
How?...
[] Spent time in nature
[] Listened to my favourite song
[] Ate something healthy
[] Called a friend
[] Hugged someone
[] Completed an unfinished task. What was
   it?...
[] Started/worked on a hobby
[] Read a few pages of a great book
[] Took photos of something beautiful
[] Started to learn a new skill
[] Laughed at something really funny

Today was fun
because..
....
....

Happiness rating:

1 2 3 4 5 6 7 8 9 10

Day 349

I am grateful for:

1...
....

2...
....

3...
....

Today I:

[] Did 15 minutes of exercise
[] Sat quietly and relaxed (meditation)
[] Was kind to someone.
How?..
[] Spent time in nature
[] Listened to my favourite song
[] Ate something healthy
[] Called a friend
[] Hugged someone
[] Completed an unfinished task. What was
   it?......................................
[] Started/worked on a hobby
[] Read a few pages of a great book
[] Took photos of something beautiful
[] Started to learn a new skill
[] Laughed at something really funny

Today was fun
because......................................
....
....

Happiness rating:

        1 2 3 4 5 6 7 8 9 10

Day 350

I am grateful for:

1..
....

2..
....

3..
....

Today I:

[] Did 15 minutes of exercise
[] Sat quietly and relaxed (meditation)
[] Was kind to someone.
How?......................................
[] Spent time in nature
[] Listened to my favourite song
[] Ate something healthy
[] Called a friend
[] Hugged someone
[] Completed an unfinished task. What was
    it?....................................
[] Started/worked on a hobby
[] Read a few pages of a great book
[] Took photos of something beautiful
[] Started to learn a new skill
[] Laughed at something really funny

Today was fun
because...................................
....
....

Happiness rating:

 1 2 3 4 5 6 7 8 9 10

412

Ripples...

As your happiness grows, your life will get better and better. You will smile and laugh more. Appreciate more. Give more. Do more. Be more.

This can't just have an impact on you!

Each act of kindness, every smile, every happy thought or burst of laughter will have a positive effect on those around you. They will be happier, and in turn make decisions that will improve their lives and the lives of those around them.
The smallest act of kindness toward someone can start a ripple.

A ripple that spreads far and wide like those from a tiny pebble dropped into a pond.

This ripple effect will happen whether your actions are positive or negative!

So, every time you decide between a positive or negative thought, feeling or action, remember your ripples!

Jeff Olson (2013 Kindle Edition), *The Slight Edge.*

Day 351

I am grateful for:

1..
....

2..
....

3..
....

Today I:

[] Did 15 minutes of exercise
[] Sat quietly and relaxed (meditation)
[] Was kind to someone.
How?......................................
[] Spent time in nature
[] Listened to my favourite song
[] Ate something healthy
[] Called a friend
[] Hugged someone
[] Completed an unfinished task. What was
   it?......................................
[] Started/worked on a hobby
[] Read a few pages of a great book
[] Took photos of something beautiful
[] Started to learn a new skill
[] Laughed at something really funny

Today was fun
because...................................
....
....

Happiness rating:

1   2   3   4   5   6   7   8   9   10

Day 352

I am grateful for:
1...
....
2...
....
3...
....

Today I:

[] Did 15 minutes of exercise
[] Sat quietly and relaxed (meditation)
[] Was kind to someone.
How?.......................................
[] Spent time in nature
[] Listened to my favourite song
[] Ate something healthy
[] Called a friend
[] Hugged someone
[] Completed an unfinished task. What was
   it?.....................................
[] Started/worked on a hobby
[] Read a few pages of a great book
[] Took photos of something beautiful
[] Started to learn a new skill
[] Laughed at something really funny

Today was fun
because....................................
....
....

Happiness rating:

    1 2 3 4 5 6 7 8 9 10

Day 353

I am grateful for:

1..
....
2..
....
3..
....

Today I:

[] Did 15 minutes of exercise
[] Sat quietly and relaxed (meditation)
[] Was kind to someone.
How?...
[] Spent time in nature
[] Listened to my favourite song
[] Ate something healthy
[] Called a friend
[] Hugged someone
[] Completed an unfinished task. What was
   it?..
[] Started/worked on a hobby
[] Read a few pages of a great book
[] Took photos of something beautiful
[] Started to learn a new skill
[] Laughed at something really funny

Today was fun
because......................................
....
....

Happiness rating:

         1 2 3 4 5 6 7 8 9 10

Day 354

I am grateful for:

1...
....

2...
....

3...
....

Today I:

[] Did 15 minutes of exercise
[] Sat quietly and relaxed (meditation)
[] Was kind to someone.
How?...
[] Spent time in nature
[] Listened to my favourite song
[] Ate something healthy
[] Called a friend
[] Hugged someone
[] Completed an unfinished task. What was
    it?.......................................
[] Started/worked on a hobby
[] Read a few pages of a great book
[] Took photos of something beautiful
[] Started to learn a new skill
[] Laughed at something really funny

Today was fun
because.......................................
....
....

Happiness rating:

        1   2   3   4   5   6   7   8   9   10

417

Day 355

I am grateful for:

1..
....

2..
....

3..
....

Today I:

[] Did 15 minutes of exercise
[] Sat quietly and relaxed (meditation)
[] Was kind to someone.
How?......................................
[] Spent time in nature
[] Listened to my favourite song
[] Ate something healthy
[] Called a friend
[] Hugged someone
[] Completed an unfinished task. What was
   it?......................................
[] Started/worked on a hobby
[] Read a few pages of a great book
[] Took photos of something beautiful
[] Started to learn a new skill
[] Laughed at something really funny

Today was fun
because....................................
....
....

Happiness rating:

    1 2 3 4 5 6 7 8 9 10

Day 356

I am grateful for:

1..
....

2..
....

3..
....

Today I:

[] Did 15 minutes of exercise
[] Sat quietly and relaxed (meditation)
[] Was kind to someone.
How?..
[] Spent time in nature
[] Listened to my favourite song
[] Ate something healthy
[] Called a friend
[] Hugged someone
[] Completed an unfinished task. What was
   it?.....................................
[] Started/worked on a hobby
[] Read a few pages of a great book
[] Took photos of something beautiful
[] Started to learn a new skill
[] Laughed at something really funny

Today was fun
because.....................................
....
....

Happiness rating:

1 2 3 4 5 6 7 8 9 10

Day 357

I am grateful for:
1..
....
2..
....
3..
....

Today I:

[] Did 15 minutes of exercise
[] Sat quietly and relaxed (meditation)
[] Was kind to someone.
How?..
[] Spent time in nature
[] Listened to my favourite song
[] Ate something healthy
[] Called a friend
[] Hugged someone
[] Completed an unfinished task. What was
    it?..
[] Started/worked on a hobby
[] Read a few pages of a great book
[] Took photos of something beautiful
[] Started to learn a new skill
[] Laughed at something really funny

Today was fun
because...
....
....

Happiness rating:

        1   2   3   4   5   6   7   8   9   10

___

Watch your input
Choosing your influence

The people you choose, books you read, media you watch and games you play can all add up and have a massive impact on your happiness.

There is a lot of negativity in the media... much more than there is positivity. You don't have to watch it. You don't have to listen to it. And you don't have to talk about it. Spreading negativity doesn't actually make the world better. Try watching, listening to, and talking about good news as much as you can.

What's your entertainment like? Is it mostly sad, depressing or violent? Or funny, happy and uplifting? I'm not saying to never ever watch a sad movie, read a scary book, or play a war game on your Xbox, just take notice of how you feel afterwards, and make sure you have a balance that weighs towards the positive...

Most importantly are your people. Who do you choose to look up to? Whose stories inspire you? Find happy people (either in person or through books and media) who you can aspire to be like. How do they behave, speak and move? What are their happiness habits? Do you feel uplifted and happy after reading about them or spending time with them? Gravitate towards people who bring out your best and happiest self. Share your life with people who are generous, loving and happy!

Day 358

I am grateful for:

1...
....

2...
....

3...
....

Today I:

[] Did 15 minutes of exercise
[] Sat quietly and relaxed (meditation)
[] Was kind to someone.
How?...
[] Spent time in nature
[] Listened to my favourite song
[] Ate something healthy
[] Called a friend
[] Hugged someone
[] Completed an unfinished task. What was
   it?.......................................
[] Started/worked on a hobby
[] Read a few pages of a great book
[] Took photos of something beautiful
[] Started to learn a new skill
[] Laughed at something really funny

Today was fun
because......................................
....
....

Happiness rating:

1   2   3   4   5   6   7   8   9   10

Day 359

I am grateful for:

1..
....

2..
....

3..
....

Today I:

[] Did 15 minutes of exercise
[] Sat quietly and relaxed (meditation)
[] Was kind to someone.
How?.......................................
[] Spent time in nature
[] Listened to my favourite song
[] Ate something healthy
[] Called a friend
[] Hugged someone
[] Completed an unfinished task. What was
    it?......................................
[] Started/worked on a hobby
[] Read a few pages of a great book
[] Took photos of something beautiful
[] Started to learn a new skill
[] Laughed at something really funny

Today was fun
because.....................................
....
....

Happiness rating:

    1 2 3 4 5 6 7 8 9 10

Day 360

I am grateful for:

1...
....

2...
....

3...
....

Today I:

[] Did 15 minutes of exercise
[] Sat quietly and relaxed (meditation)
[] Was kind to someone.
How?..
[] Spent time in nature
[] Listened to my favourite song
[] Ate something healthy
[] Called a friend
[] Hugged someone
[] Completed an unfinished task. What was
   it?.......................................
[] Started/worked on a hobby
[] Read a few pages of a great book
[] Took photos of something beautiful
[] Started to learn a new skill
[] Laughed at something really funny

Today was fun
because.....................................
....
....

Happiness rating:

    1 2 3 4 5 6 7 8 9 10

Day 361

I am grateful for:
1...
....
2...
....
3...
....

Today I:

[] Did 15 minutes of exercise
[] Sat quietly and relaxed (meditation)
[] Was kind to someone.
How?......................................
[] Spent time in nature
[] Listened to my favourite song
[] Ate something healthy
[] Called a friend
[] Hugged someone
[] Completed an unfinished task. What was
    it?.....................................
[] Started/worked on a hobby
[] Read a few pages of a great book
[] Took photos of something beautiful
[] Started to learn a new skill
[] Laughed at something really funny

Today was fun
because....................................
....
....

Happiness rating:

        1 2 3 4 5 6 7 8 9 10

Day 362

I am grateful for:

1..
....

2..
....

3..
....

Today I:

[] Did 15 minutes of exercise
[] Sat quietly and relaxed (meditation)
[] Was kind to someone.
How?...
[] Spent time in nature
[] Listened to my favourite song
[] Ate something healthy
[] Called a friend
[] Hugged someone
[] Completed an unfinished task. What was
   it?..
[] Started/worked on a hobby
[] Read a few pages of a great book
[] Took photos of something beautiful
[] Started to learn a new skill
[] Laughed at something really funny

Today was fun
because.......................................
....
....

Happiness rating:

     1   2   3   4   5   6   7   8   9   10

Day 363

I am grateful for:

1..
....

2..
....

3..
....

Today I:

[] Did 15 minutes of exercise
[] Sat quietly and relaxed (meditation)
[] Was kind to someone.
How?......................................
[] Spent time in nature
[] Listened to my favourite song
[] Ate something healthy
[] Called a friend
[] Hugged someone
[] Completed an unfinished task. What was
   it?....................................
[] Started/worked on a hobby
[] Read a few pages of a great book
[] Took photos of something beautiful
[] Started to learn a new skill
[] Laughed at something really funny

Today was fun
because...................................
....
....

Happiness rating:

1   2   3   4   5   6   7   8   9   10

Day 364

I am grateful for:

1..
....

2..
....

3..
....

Today I:

[] Did 15 minutes of exercise
[] Sat quietly and relaxed (meditation)
[] Was kind to someone.
How?..
[] Spent time in nature
[] Listened to my favourite song
[] Ate something healthy
[] Called a friend
[] Hugged someone
[] Completed an unfinished task. What was
   it?.......................................
[] Started/worked on a hobby
[] Read a few pages of a great book
[] Took photos of something beautiful
[] Started to learn a new skill
[] Laughed at something really funny

Today was fun
because.....................................
....
....

Happiness rating:

1   2   3   4   5   6   7   8   9   10

Day 365

I am grateful for:
1..
....
2..
....
3..
....

Today I:

[] Did 15 minutes of exercise
[] Sat quietly and relaxed (meditation)
[] Was kind to someone.
How?...
[] Spent time in nature
[] Listened to my favourite song
[] Ate something healthy
[] Called a friend
[] Hugged someone
[] Completed an unfinished task. What was
   it?...
[] Started/worked on a hobby
[] Read a few pages of a great book
[] Took photos of something beautiful
[] Started to learn a new skill
[] Laughed at something really funny

Today was fun
because..
....
....

Happiness rating:

       1 2 3 4 5 6 7 8 9 10

You've done it!
365 days of everyday
happiness...

Time To

Celebrate!

(Party time)

Keep Reading

Reading is great. A good book can take you places, ignite your imagination, teach you, and even provide friendship and a place of freedom when you need it.

We generally read different things for different reasons.
Great novels to escape to another world.
Comic books for a laugh.
Magazines for the latest trends and gossip.
Blogs, newspapers and non-fiction books to help us learn and grow.
And inspiring books to motivate, influence and encourage us to make positive change.

Reading provides stimulation for your brain, keeping it active and engaged. It has a positive impact on your education or work by increasing your knowledge, expanding your vocabulary, giving you a stronger memory and thinking skills and improving your focus and concentration. You will probably also become better at writing. All this can amount to improved confidence and self-esteem.

Whether it is to entertain, inspire, distract or inform, what you decide to read can have an impact on your happiness. Books, comics and blogs can be a great source of laughter and happiness. And even a sad book can have a positive influence, allowing us to label and vent our negative emotions.

Non-fiction books and biographies can be inspiring. You can learn about anyone and anything, and use what you learn in your own life.
With a novel we can even escape into other worlds and distract ourselves from our own worries.

Reading also informs and educates us about our world and the people in it. Be careful though: consistently reading 'real life' news can have a negative effect, as there is a lot more bad news reported than good. (For every bad news story reported there are thousands of good stories not reported!)

Hint
Don't worry if you're not 'into' reading. Just a few pages of an excellent book every day adds up to an education.

(In this case it's HAPPINESS!)

"Reading is to the mind what exercise is to the body."

Joseph Addison

You are
enough
just as you
are...

You are
capable,
acceptable
and
amazing...

You are free
to be whoever
you choose!

You are free
to be
happy!

"Every end is a new beginning."

Marianne Williamson.

...So what are you going to do now...?

References

(Quote) *The Adventures of Sharkboy and Lavagirl* (2005). Directed by Robert Rodriguez, Columbia Pictures.

(Quote) *Happy* (2013). Pharrell Williams, Black Lot Music, Columbia.

Raising Happiness (2011). Christine Carter, Random House Inc.

The Happy Secret to Better Work (2011). Shawn Achor, TED Talk, www.ted.com.

Positive Psychology and the Science of Happiness (2016). No author listed, www.pursuit-of-happiness.org.

The Science of Setting Goals (2014). Nadia Goodman, interview with Kelly McGonigal, www.ideas.ted.com.

(Quote) *The Lego Movie* (2014). Directed by Phil Lord and Christopher Miller, Warner Brothers Pictures.

Thanks! How The New Science of Gratitude can make you Happier (2007). Robert Emmons, Houghton Mifflin Harcourt.

(Quote) *Oh, The Places You'll Go!* (1990). Dr Seuss, Random House.

Exercise (2016). No author listed, www.pursuit-of-happiness.org.

Unlimited Power (2001 Edition). Tony Robbins,
Pocket Books.

The One And Only Thing you need to be Happy (2012). Tony Robbins,
https://training.tonyrobbins.com.

What is Meditation? (ND).
https://thebuddhistcentre.com.

7 Reasons Why Teens Should Meditate (ND).
Ariana Marini, choices.scholastic.com.

How to Get Kids to Meditate (ND).
Bess O'Connor, chopra.com

(Quote) 3rd Law of Physics. Isaac Newton.

(Quote) Evan Almighty (2007). Directed by Tom Shadyac, Universal Pictures.

(Quote) William James, American Philosopher and Psychologist, 1842-1910.

*(Quote) Harry Potter and The Prisoner of Azkaban (*1999). J.K. Rowling, Bloomsbury.

(Quote) Mr Magorium's Wonder Emporium (2007). Directed by Zach Helm, UK: Icon Productions

Immerse yourself in a forest for better health (ND). Department of Environmental Health, www.dec.ny.gov.

Health Benefits of Nature (ND), American Society of Landscape Architects, www.asla.org.

How Music Affects Our Moods (2013).
Suzanne Boothby (quoting Yuna Ferguson),
www.healthline.com.

How Does Music Affect Teenagers' Emotions?
(2013). Jae Allen, www.livestrong.com.

(Quote) Hans Christian Anderson. Source:
www.goodreads.com.

(Quote) *Come From the Heart* (song,1987).
Suzanna Clarke, Richard Leigh,
quoteinvestigator.com.

Six Foods That Make You Happier (2015).
Cynthia Sass, news.health.com.

(Quote) Charles Schulz, author of *Peanuts*.
Source: www.goodreads.com.

*10 Keys To Happier Living - Family And
Friends* (ND). www.actionforhappiness.org.

(Quote) Amanda Bradley.

The Secret of Happiness (2013). Tony
Robbins, Youtube.com.

(Quote) Tony Robbins.

The Slight Edge (2013 Kindle Edition). Jeff
Olson, Greenleaf Book Press.

7 Benefits of Having a Hobby (2013). Dani
Dipirro, www.positivelypresent.com.

(Quote) *Finding Nemo* (2003). Directed by
Andrew Stanton, Buena Vista Pictures.

The Most Inspiring Famous Failures (2013).
Ruben Garcia, blog.megafounder.com.

(Quote) Harvard Commencement Address (2008).
J.K. Rowling, harvardmagazine.com.

Decisions (2013). Tony Robbins,
www.youtube.com.

(Quote) Feel the fear and do it anyway
(2006). Susan Jeffers, Ballantine Books

*Using Mindful Photography to Increase
Positive Emotion and Appreciation* (2013).
Jaime L. Kurtz and Sonja Lyubomirsky,
American Psychological Association.

(Quote) Earth From Above (2005). Yann
Arthus-Bertrand, Harry N Abrams Inc.

The Call of Solitude (1998, reviewed 2012).
Ester Buchholz, www.psychologytoday.com.

The Health Benefits of Dogs (and Cats)
(2016). Lawrence Robinson and Jeanne Segal
Ph.D., www.helpguide.org.

*(Quote) Marley & Me: Life and Times with the
Worlds Worst Dog* (2007). John Grogan, Hodder
and Stoughton.

Laughter is the Best Medicine (2016).
Melinda Smith MA and Jeanne Segal Ph.D.,
www.helpguide.org.

(Quote) Katrina Mayer, PhD Author and
inspirational speaker (among other things).
katrinamayer.com.

(Quote) *We Bought a Zoo* (2011). Directed By Cameron Crowe, 20th Century Fox.

(Quote) Joseph Addison, English writer and politician (1672-1719).

(Quote) *Everyday Grace* (2002). Marianne Williamson, Riverhead Books.

Printed in Great Britain
by Amazon